GIFTS
OF OUR
FATHERS

Heartfelt Remembrances of
Fathers and Grandfathers

Edited by Thomas R. Verny

Photographs by Marianne Gontarz

by Unity Library

UNITY SCHOOL LIBRARY
UNITY VILLAGE, MISSOURI 64065

The Crossing Press • Freedom, CA 95019

6/95

Library of Congress Cataloging-in-Publication Data

Gifts of our fathers: heartfelt remembrances of fathers &
    grandfathers / edited by Thomas R. Verny; photographs by Marianne
    Gontarz
        p.   cm.
    ISBN 0-89594-659-9.   —   ISBN 0-89594-658-0   (pbk.)
    1. Fathers.   2. Grandfathers.   I. Verny, Thomas R.
HQ756.G495   1994
306.874'2 —dc20   93-40382

V

In loving memory of my father, Eugene Verny,
and my grandfather, Leopold Neufeld.

Table of Contents

Introduction   1

Fathers Day • *Mark Greenside*   7

Daddy, We Called You • *Maria Mazziotti Gillan*   13

Tomato Soup Feeling • *Jessica Lee*   18

And Andrew His Brother • *Marion Woodman*   21

Re-inventing the Archives • *Elisavietta Ritchie*   29

War-Gone • *C.B. Follett*   45

The Worst Business • *Peter Such*   47

Prayer for My Father • *Robert Bly*   57

A Pot Full of Green Beans • *Mike Lipstock*   59

Close Tolerances • *William J. Smart*   65

The Tower Room • *C.B. Follett*   74

Buddies • *Mary M. Alward*   76

My Father at Eighty-Five • *Robert Bly*   82

Grandfather's Watch • *Thomas R. Verny*   84

There Is Nothing Wrong With Being Afraid

    • *Elisabeth Spaude Aubrey*   92

Conversion • *Charlotte C. Gordon*   101

My Father's Gold Tooth • *Sandra Collier*   104

Not Here • *C.B. Follet*   113

Between a Father and Son • *Peter C. Samu*   116

The Spiny Beast • *Robert Bly*   129

Daddy's Chair • *Mary M. Alward*   132

My Three Fathers • *Valentina Bek*   140

Permission • *Richard Cole*   162

Abuelo Cesar Ate With His Fingers • *Janice Levy*   163

Play Me A Song • *Joan Hoekstra*   169

Portrait of a Lawyer as a Young Dad • *Janet Hutchinson*   176

My Father's Neck • *Robert Bly*   186

Send Flowers To The Nurses • *Nancy Robertson*   188

Contributors   197

Introduction

Fathers and grandfathers seem to bestow upon their children both precious gifts and painful wounds. I was reminded of this last July when a friend of mine offered to read me a story about his father. My friend Peter is a radiologist, kind to a fault but emotionally reserved. I was, therefore, quite unprepared for some of the deeply moving passages in his story. In fact, it brought tears to my eyes several times. "Have you thought of getting this story published?" I asked him after I finished reading it. "No, who would ever want to read it?" he responded in his usual dyspeptic way. For several days after I could not put his story out of my mind. Finally, it came to me. I would publish my friend's story in a book of short stories about fathers and grandfathers written by their own sons and daughters.

As I thought more about this project I gradually developed basic guidelines for the proposed anthology. I decided to collect original, previously unpublished stories because I did not think it fair that a reader would purchase a book only to discover that he was already familiar with a couple of the stories in the book. I stipulated that the stories be authentic in the sense of being based on true events. In order to avoid being bored to death with *Reader's Digest* type the-day-my-father-taught-me-fly-fishing stories I specified that the stories be emotionally moving, intellectually challenging and follow the shape, structure and literary traditions of a finely crafted work of short fiction.

After I arrived at a general understanding of the kind of stories I would like to collect I asked myself: Is there a real need for this book? Apart from being entertaining will it serve a deeper purpose?

Only a hermit would be unaware of the fact that men have been getting a lot of bad press lately. And deservedly so. However, it seems to me that for every man who abuses children, violates women and pollutes the environment there are countless others who love, nurture and support their families, friends and fellow human beings. Perhaps it's time men and women be reminded of that.

As men have become an endangered species it seems to be desirable to redress the balance and to realize that many of us have profoundly benefited from our male ancestors. However, the last thing I wanted in the book were tributes, odes, homages or eulogies full of piety and sweet insincerities. The stories that I sought were not meant to be inspirational in the conventional sense; rather, they were to be about real people: the bright and the dark side.

Even if there was but one shining moment, a genuine expression of love, in an otherwise bleak relationship, I was open to having that story in the book. Furthermore, I wanted the stories to deal not only with the father or grandfather but also with the relationship, the ebb and flow of feelings between them; how each affected the other and changed as a result.

We all know people who received very little love from their fathers but plenty of sarcasm, shaming, blaming and belittling. It is difficult for such individuals to become warm and caring mothers and fathers when their turn comes to parent their children. It occurred to me that by reading the stories and poems in this book perhaps some of the open wounds in one's emotional body may be healed and some of the father hunger in our bellies may be stilled.

The majority of the contributors are accomplished writers whose works have frequently appeared in literary magazines and anthologies. Some are highly acclaimed and popular writers such as Robert Bly, Maria Mazziotti Gillan, Peter Such, Elisavietta Ritchie and Marion Woodman to name but a few, while others have not been published before. I think the latter group is an integral part of this book because what it may lack in polish and verbal virtuosity it makes up for in honesty and depth of feeling. A brief biography of each author appears at the back of the book.

The sense of missed opportunities to connect, the inability to speak one's deepest feelings is a frequent theme in many of the stories. In "Your Missal" the author searches through her father's prayer book for

> "...something. A letter. A note. A scrawl. Something
> that says you love me."

Jessica Lee in a tiny gem of a story entitled "Tomato Soup Feeling" puts it this way:

> "And he takes a spoon and fills it with soup. And he blows on it so it won't burn a little throat already raw... I know if he could he would tell me that he loves me. If kisses were his style he would give me a big one. But he gives me more soup and his eyes are wet and full of fear and hope and I get that tomato soup feeling again."

In an age in which the media seldom focus on fathers' or grandfathers' moral authority, courage, integrity, strength, patience, empathy or warmth it seems to me particularly important to be reminded that men with such qualities really do exist. These stories and poems show us that good fathering is not extinct.

Elisavietta Ritchie in "Re-inventing the Archives" writes about her father.

> "What stories he told. I grew up wishing I had more of my own to tell, and cursing my own life for being so—relatively—simple, comfortable, safe. Daddy often quoted Alfred de Vigny: 'One must live in the flames.' Have I spent my life searching for sparks?
>
> He discourses hours on any subject with brilliance, and knowledge. What he doesn't know, he finds out. He is kinder and more generous than anyone I've ever met. And more energetic: he will swim a river and hike a mountain before breakfast, work all day, sing and dance all night—the life of the party.
>
> That is: when he was younger. Healthier. Before his hands developed a tremor, tools began to slip from his fingers, a stroll to the mailbox exhausted him. He misplaced bills, keys, names. In the middle of a dance he forgot how to tango."

I think all of us want our fathers and grandfathers to be larger than life. We expect them to be heroic and virtuous. We wish that at the end of their earthly sojourn they would echo Marion Woodman's father, "Lord, I have fought a good fight, I have finished my course, I have kept the faith."

As I read the poems and stories that appear in this book I gleaned fresh insights into my own relationships with my grandfather and father as well as my children and grandchildren. This was not always a pleasant experience. Indeed, the process of illuminating the dark corners of one's soul can be quite disturbing at times. Yet in the long run, I found it liberating and empowering and I hope they will similarly affect the reader.

There is one other thing. Though the subject matter of this book is fathers and grandfathers this is not "a book for men." The majority of contributors are women and I believe that the book will engage both men and women. *Gifts of Our Fathers* is not about sexual politics, the sociology of the family, or the psychology of men. It is about being a daughter or a son, about being or becoming a mother or a father, a grandmother or a grandfather. It is about our struggle to be fully human.

Thomas R. Verny
Spring, 1993

GIFTS OF OUR FATHERS

Father's Day

Mark Greenside

It astonishes me, the relationship between kids and their parents. You take a guy, an average guy, someone with nothing outstanding going for him— he may not even be nice. And there by his side is his kid. All this kid wants is this guy's eye; his hand; a look; a hint; a whisper of some recognition. The guy touches the kid, rubs his head, takes his hand, and the kid looks at him as if he's in heaven.

I'm standing here in Grand Central Station seeing this. All around me the place is a zoo. Crazy people, wackos, weirdos, loonies, junkies, refugees from every sore and wound in the world, screeching at each other, babbling in words, sounds, grunts, gestures, pushing, humping, bumping, shoving for this reason or that or no reason. It's monstrous. Terrible. Frightening. It's an inferno—and this kid, this babe, this lamb, this innocent, feels safe because this guy is standing there right next to him. Nobody else in the world—not the guy's mother, not his wife, nobody—would find comfort in his being there. Some people move further away from him. He just feels vulnerable. If anybody's going to get hit this afternoon, he knows it's going to be him. But this kid—this seven-year-old boy—feels protected from God, the world, insanity, nature, from anything and everything as it all takes place in front of him beneath the grand stairway leading down from the stars. This kid looks up and sees none of it. He holds his father's hand and looks at him as if he's a hero with holy, unqualified love. It amazes me. I'm awestruck at the power, the authority, the grace children believe their parents have. It must be the reason people have kids.

I'm thinking about this because it's Father's Day. I've been thinking about my dad a lot. He was a big man, over six feet tall, and he had large hands and long fingers that were thick and strong. I remember how he used to toss me high in the air and catch me and put me on his shoulders and run. Mom would always run around after us, laughing, and saying, "Careful, Joe, be careful." "Careful," when we wrestled. "Careful," when we played ball. "Careful, careful, don't be so hard and rough." But of course he never was hard and rough, and he never hurt me either.

I remember once when I was six looking into their bedroom and seeing my dad in his underwear standing in front of the mirror, flexing and strutting around. Mom saw me and giggled, then called me. "Come here, Jay—come here and feel your daddy's muscles." Dad made a muscle and lifted me up with one arm, then he put me down and kissed me on the top of my head. It was about noon then and we'd just finished a late Sunday breakfast. I can still see him now as he winked at my mom, the way he always did when they had a secret. He knelt down and put his hands on my shoulders. "Want to go out for a ride?" he asked. "Just the two of us. Just the men."

"Yeah!" I yelled and started to jump up and down. I loved going driving with my dad. He'd put the top down no matter how cold it was and we'd go out to the beltway and speed. I grabbed my Giants hat and a jacket and ran to my room to get ready. The car we had then was a 1956 Thunderbird. It was two years old but a beauty and dad kept it in tip-top shape. We washed and vacuumed it every other weekend and polished it with Turtle Wax three times a year: in the summer, fall, and spring. In the winter dad wouldn't even drive it because of the snow and salt on the roads. He locked it in a garage and started it once a week to keep the fluids moving and the battery alive. Mom said we couldn't afford the car or the garage, but she loved it as much as he did, I think, and was just as happy that we had it.

I got ready first and waited outside for my dad. I walked around the T-Bird and looked at it. I knew I wasn't supposed to get in. That was one of dad's rules for keeping it looking new: I couldn't eat or drink in the car because if I spilled it would ruin the interior; I couldn't touch the windows because my hands left grease marks that were hard to remove; and never, ever, under any circumstances could I sit on the car or lean against it or rest packages or schoolbooks or keys or baseball gloves or anything else on the fenders, hood, or trunk because the paint could easily scratch or chip. So I sat down on the grass and waited a few feet from the car with my jacket and hat in my lap and listened as the door opened and watched him as he kissed my mom goodbye and came down the stairs with a smile. "How's my baby?" he said, running his hand along the black canvas top of the car. He always did that when he took the T-Bird out for a ride. He called the car his baby, mom was his babe, and I was his big sonny boy.

He unlocked his door and opened mine and together we unfastened the top and lowered it, making sure it didn't catch or crimp as we folded it down. Then he took one side and I took the other and we snapped the red cover down over the top. It was a warm, sunny autumn day, perfect for a drive. I got into the car and sat next to the window, where mom usually sat, and watched dad as he walked around and examined the tires.

"Are you ready?" he finally asked. I nodded. He reached over and locked my door. Then he turned the key and smiled again as the engine caught and went vrooom. While the car warmed up dad put on his mirrored sun-glasses, the type that you can't see a person's eyes through. He took a cig-arette from a pack of Camels, tapped it on the back of his hand, and placed it between his lips. Then he twisted the rearview mirror so he could see himself and he took out his comb and began combing his hair. When he was done and the engine was warm, he put the mirror back in place, lit his cigarette, and inhaled. I always thought of him as my dad, but I think he saw himself as a young Bogie or James Dean. He blew out the smoke and reached over and rubbed my head. "Let's go get 'em," he said, "you and me," and he slid the T-Bird into reverse.

We headed out towards the beltway. It was beautiful out, clear and dry, with a warm wind blowing in our faces. I had to hold on to my cap. We had the radio on and we were singing along with the music. In the dis-tance, I saw the sign for our cutoff. Dad saw it too and he pushed his foot down on the accelerator. The car picked up speed with ease. We must have been doing seventy, seventy-five miles an hour. We turned the radio up and the heat on and sang louder. It seemed like we were the only car on the road. "Hey," dad yelled, so I could hear him over the wind and the radio, "do you know what today is?" I shook my head yes and said, "Sunday." Dad laughed. "That's right, my big sonny boy, it's *Son*-day…" and I giggled because I got it. "It's a day for fathers and sons." Then he put his arm around me and squeezed.

We were moving along at over eighty now and heading out towards the beach where the traffic was thinner and we could safely speed. "See that car way up there?" dad pointed. "See how far away it is?" I nodded. "Why don't you count and see how long it takes to pass him?" I started counting and in no time at all, maybe ten seconds, we moved past him like he was standing still. "Get a horse," dad yelled, and we laughed and waved our arms and howled into the wind as the speedometer needle moved past ninety.

We drove on like that for a while, until the road became straight and empty—a perfect place to let go. Dad accelerated and pushed the car close to a hundred, then over a hundred. The speedometer itself went up to one-hundred-and-twenty. The fastest I'd ever gone was one-ten. We were now at a hundred and three. We were flying. That's what it felt like: flying. The radio was on full blast and I could barely hear it. We were moving so fast I could hardly see. There was just us and the wind and the car and the road… Dad pushed… One-O-Seven… One-Ten… One-Twelve… Thirteen. Fourteen… The car shook—dad hesitated. I could feel him lift his foot from the pedal. "Are you scared?" he yelled. "No," I said, and seeing he couldn't hear me I shook my head and shouted, "No, not a bit." Dad nodded and pushed his foot down and the T-Bird surged ahead… One-thirteen, fourteen, fifteen, seventeen, nineteen… At one-twenty the needle hovered. It held there… Lingered… we watched it, we waited—and when it finally crossed the mark we hollered and yelled, "We did it! We did it! We did it!" Then dad took his foot off the pedal and let the car slow down to sixty. It felt like we were standing still. At the next cutoff he turned around and we headed home.

On the ride back one of us would occasionally say something about "breaking the limit" or "crossing the barrier," but most of the time we were quiet. We were exhilarated, full of ourselves and what we accomplished. We felt brave and strong like ancient gods and conquering heroes. We had been tested and we passed the test. Down the road, way ahead, I saw the car we had passed earlier. We drove past it again and waved. The guy waved back, then pulled ahead of us, and with no warning at all cut us off. Dad jammed on the brakes and turned the wheel hard to avoid hitting him. I hit my head on the dash. "You OK?" dad asked, "you OK?" and he reached over and touched my head. It hurt a little —there was a small bump already, I could feel it—but I wasn't really hurt and I told him so. Yes, I nodded, "I'm OK." "Shit," dad cursed. "That asshole. The stupid son of a bitch." Then he peeled out and pulled even with the guy and stared at him for a long time and called him a "jerk." The guy stared back, then dropped behind us. Sitting next to him, I saw, was a kid.

We drove on like that for a while, keeping an eye on him and then forgetting him, until we finally came to our exit. We turned off. The guy followed and as we stopped at a stop sign he pulled around us and blocked the car. Dad and I watched as he got out of his car—a rusty and dented old Chevy—and stood by his open door. He was older than my dad, in his thirties, and shorter and wiry looking. He was wearing pressed dungarees, a Yankees cap, and a white T-shirt, and he hadn't shaved in a couple of days. He lifted his cap and ran his fingers through his hair, then walked around to the back of his car and put his hands on the T-Bird's hood. Dad looked at me and got out of the car. "Who the fuck do you think you are?" the guy started screaming. "What the fuck are you doing? Where the fuck are you going?" Dad tried to calm him down, but the guy got louder and louder. Each time he said something he pushed down hard on the car and made it bounce. Dad was talking too, but I couldn't hear him. Finally, the guy slapped the hood of the T-Bird with his palm and walked away. Dad got back in the car furious, cursing, calling the guy crazy, an idiot, nuts, a moron, and wrote down his license plate number as soon as the guy drove away. I watched as dad wrote, watched his fingers, watched his hand, his writing, the way the numbers and letters came out broken and bent, tore through the paper, and went way outside of the lines, and I looked at his face and I saw it, and I'll never forget it, though I never saw it that way again—he was scared. Really scared. Frightened... My dad was frightened. The same way I was scared of the night, the dark, of going to sleep and being attacked by ghosts. Scared white. Scared green. Scared red. Scared silly. Scared so bad he turned to me and said, "Guess we showed him, huh, big fella!"

I nodded.

"Sometimes, you know, it's smarter to walk away."

I turned away, then heard a slap and turned back and saw dad punching his fist into his palm. "Sure would have liked to have belted him, though... Were you scared?"

Unh huh, I shook my head.

"No? Not just a little?"

Unh huh.

"What if I'd hit him and he pulled a knife?"

"I'd have hit him hard, in the head, with a rock."

We looked at each other then and we broke out laughing because each of us knew we were lying. Dad reached out and touched my head, kissed the bump, and held me. "Let's not tell mom how this happened," he said.

I looked at him, surprised. "How come?"

"She'll only worry about us next time we go out. She'll think when we go places we fight."

So I never did. I never told my mother or my sister or my wife—or anyone else all these years. It's a secret I've kept for my dad. And the truth is I hardly ever recall it. It's something that hardly matters at all, except at certain times and places like at Grand Central Station when I'm standing with my son and I'm afraid that someone will say something or do something or something will happen and I won't be able to pretend that it didn't, and I'll have to act, and I'll be petrified, and I wonder: Is today the day I fall from grace?

Daddy, We Called You

Maria Mazziotti Gillan

"Daddy," we called you, "Daddy"
when we talked to each other in the street,
pulling on our American faces,
shaping our lives in Paterson slang.

Inside our house, we spoke
a Southern Italian dialect
mixed with English
and we called you "Papa,"

but outside again, you became Daddy
and we spoke of you to our friends
as "my father,"
imagining we were speaking
of that "Father Knows Best"
TV character
in his dark business suit,
carrying his briefcase into his house,
retreating to his paneled den,
his big living room and dining room,
his frilly-aproned wife
who greeted him at the door
with a kiss. Such space
and silence in that house

and ours, so crowded.
In our apartment, we lived
in one big room—living room,
dining room, kitchen, bedroom,
all in one, dominated by the gray oak dining table
around which we sat, talking and laughing,
listening to your stories,
your political arguments with your friends,

Papa, how you glowed in company light,
happy when the other Italians
came to you for help with their taxes
or legal papers.

It was only outside the glowing circle
that I denied you, denied your long hours
as night watchman in Royal Machine Shop.
One night, riding home from a date,
my middle class, American boyfriend
kissed me at the light; I looked up
and met your eyes as you stood at the corner

near Royal Machine. It was nearly midnight.
January. Cold and windy. You were waiting
for the bus, the streetlight illuminating
your face. I pretended I did not see you,
let my boyfriend pull away, leaving you
on the empty corner waiting for the bus
to take you home. You never mentioned it,
never said that you knew
how often I lied about what you did for a living
or that I was ashamed to have my boyfriend see you,
find out about your second shift work, your broken English.

Today, remembering that moment,
still illuminated in my mind
by the streetlamp's gray light,
I think of my own son
and the distance between us,
greater than miles.

Papa,
silk worker,
janitor,
night watchman,
immigrant Italian,

I honor the years you spent in menial work
slipping down the ladder
as your body failed you
while your mind, so quick and sharp,
longed to escape,

honor the times you got out of bed
after sleeping only an hour,
to take me to school or pick me up;
the warm bakery rolls you bought for me
on the way home from the night shift.

the letters
you wrote
to the editors
of local newspapers,
your grasp of politics
that cut past rhetoric
to find the truth
hidden in its veil of words.

Papa, better than any "Father Knows Best" father,
bland as steamed rice,
with your winepress in the cellar,
with the newspapers you collected
out of garbage piles to turn into money
you banked for us,
with your mouse traps,
with your cracked and calloused hands,
with your yellowed teeth.

Papa,
silk worker,
janitor,
night watchman,
immigrant Italian,
dragging your dead leg
through the factories of Paterson,
I am outside the house now,
shouting your name.

Tomato Soup Feeling

Jessica Lee

Maybe I learned about loving other people from my mother, but I learned about being loved from my father. Ask me what it feels like to be loved and I will tell you it's hard to explain but I can tell you what it looks like. It comes wrapped in a red and white label from an old tomato soup can…

I am seven years old, sick and in bed. Not in my own bed—too sick for that. I am in my parents' bed. These are special circumstances.

I am very sick.

From time to time I look around the cramped little bedroom in the old farmhouse. There is just enough room between the bed and the dressers to walk sideways around them. Clothes are piled high on the homemade dressers that my grandfather built. Thin plywood dressers stained to look like real wood with drawers that never pull out right—so the clothes just pile on top.

It is cold outside and not much light can pierce through the ice on the little window. When I get better I will spend hours breathing on the ice, trying to melt it, so I can see through the glass. I'll scratch little girl tracks on the wild frost patterns and my tongue will only have to freeze to the pane once or twice before I learn the safe distance.

I am alone most of the time, but every once in a while Dad comes in from the barn to check on me. I can hear him coming from a long way off because his frozen boots make loud crunching sounds as they pound down on the hardened snow. He comes in the porch and I can hear him stomp his feet and blow his nose and cough when the first rush of warm air hits his lungs. I am too sick to cough.

His face is wet from the melting frost around his eyebrows and nose-

18

hairs and little drops of water fall on me as he looks down in my eyes and says, "Let me get you something to eat. Please. You need to eat."

I shake my head "No." I'm sick and I'm sad and I'm too young to know the danger of being so little, so sick, on a farm, so far away from a doctor. No car to make the trip to town if we had to.

My father is not a nurse, not a patient man. A part of him, however, holds a fear that something terrible might happen to any one of us three children. Even when he roars at us in a drunken rage or pulls off his belt to give us a thrashing, I know he has that fear and I think somehow that it's kind, not patient.

He doesn't know whether he should hitch the horses to the old sled and go for help or whether he should try one more time.

"Please, baby. I'll fix you something. Please try."

Normally he stirs canned tomatoes into overcooked macaroni and serves fried bologna on the side. But I can hear him in the porch again breaking the ice on the top of the milk in the old cream can. He's making me soup. Soup from a can with a red and white label.

He pulls up the pink clothes hamper that still has shirts and socks and sheets hanging crazily out of the top. He sits down on it and holds out the bowl of soup.

"Please, baby. Try. Just for me."

Didn't I know how cold it was from the inch-thick frost on the windowpanes? Didn't I sense the trouble it would take to coax the horses into frozen bridles and hitch them to the sled? Leave me alone or take me along to get help. The trouble of it all.

"Please, baby. Just a little."

And he takes a spoon and fills it with soup. And he blows on it so it won't burn a little throat already raw. And he looks down at me with a fear that is the beginning of my sense of what he is all about. I open my mouth to swallow the pain, to swallow it down and he sighs and gives me more.

I know if he could he would tell me that he loves me. If kisses were his style he would give me a big one. But he gives me more soup and his eyes are wet and full of fear and hope and I get that tomato soup feeling again.

I am loved...

It is a learned thing that time can never take away. My father didn't live nearly as long as I wanted, but he lived as long as I needed.

And Andrew His Brother

· ·

Marion Woodman

I

And Jesus, walking by the sea of Galilee, saw two brothers, Simon called
Peter, and Andrew his brother, casting a net into the sea: for they were fishers.
And he saith unto them, Follow me, and I will make you fishers of men.
And they straightway left their nets and followed him.

Matthew 4:18–20

II

Snow enveloped the hunter, the hunted, and the hound. The tracks of all
three lost themselves in the Honeyland Swamp—the Swamp, wild, wild
and free—wild enough for hunter and hound to exercise all their cunning
in pursuit of the fox, free enough for the hunter to forget he was a mortal
subject to society's laws. Resting on a hollow log, conscious only of the
bell call of his hound sounding out the fox far up the line, Andrew could
feel himself superior to the townsfolk caged in their oblong boxes, trapped
in their daily routine, fettered to a complaining wife and demanding children. And he laughed out loud at the thought of Poor Tam O'Shanter and
his sullen dame, "nursing her wrath to keep it warm." Far better to love
Maggie… or reel with Jenny… or sing with Jean! But to marry them! Och
no! To give up the nights bowsing at the nappy… and Hogmanay with Brother
Paul and the lads… and the chase! Not he! He wasn't unco fou. And he,
king of the forest, flicked the snow from his cap, whistled to a scolding squir-
rel, and moved off through the swamp with the firm grace of a deer.

III

And as he journeyed, he came near Damascus: and suddenly there shined round about him a light from heaven:

And he fell to the earth, and heard a voice saying unto him, Saul, Saul, why persecutest thou me?

…And he trembling and astonished said, Lord, what wilt thou have me to do? And the Lord said unto him, Arise and go into the city and it shall be told thee what thou must do.

…And immediately there fell from his eyes as it had been scales, and he received sight forthwith, and arose, and was baptized.

Acts 9:3, 4, 6, 18

IV

The road that leads from Damascus is ever a narrow and perplexing road. To the passionate, undisciplined spirit of young Andrew it was narrow indeed. What had Greek verbs and Hebrew texts to contribute to the conversion of mankind? And what had polished shoes and pressed black suit to add to a minister of God? Sitting at his desk in his college cell in Montreal he drummed his blunted pencil on his painfully written page. He slammed the book against the wall and rushed into the corridor in search of Cooper, Brown, or Eddie. Together they would resurrect the wilds they loved. All were brilliant storytellers and soon all four were jumping ice floes off the coast of Newfoundland. Their fiery spirits thus inflamed, they had no ice floes, no seals, no foxes. Only chamber pots! Ransacking the college, they quickly strung the pots together, slung them over the main entrance, and waited for the right person to blunder into their trap.

The years of ticking off the days before the Huron and Bruce railway would carry him home gradually drew to an end. The academic discipline had partially silenced the call of the swamp; his professors' respect replaced his cronies' frankness; his Bible supplanted his gun. One loss was irreparable. On the eve of his becoming the Reverend Andrew D. Boa, his widowed mother, steadfast, fierce in her confidence in her hunter son—died.

V

And he, Andrew, went on alone. Big of body and big of soul, he tended his flock with a devotion that evoked love and respect. Sedately he manoeuvred his black Chrysler Royal over the potholes of the town line, pulled up beside a barn, and sloshed his way through the manure.

"How are the cows milking, Mrs. Gould?"

"Oh... Rev. Boa... Oh... and me in my overalls... and reekin' o' manure! Arthur... Get out here. Arthur!"

But Mrs. Gould, and all the other Mrs. Goulds, soon forgot to be embarrassed by their preacher in their barn.

When he decided to be a factory pea weigher during the war, he became "the best damn pea weigher the Canadian Canners ever hired." If old foreman Goodfellow thought he was the master of practical jokes, he, Pea Weigher Boa, would outfox him at his own game. Goodfellow awoke from his afternoon nap to find himself the butt of his men's laughter. There lay big Jack, innocent as a baby, pillowed in wild flowers, reverently clasping goldenrod in a counterfeit of death.

Young people loved his jolly nature, his long deep belly laugh that would set a whole room rocking. They liked to perform in his plays or his concerts, and if they were sharp enough to retort to his cynical jibes they were his friends for life.

Old ladies loved their private communion with their pastor. Thoughtful enough to organize a special day to honour them, he gathered them out of their beds and chairs once a year to take them to the kirk to receive their special bouquet. They smiled sympathetically when he dropped his frosted cake or spilt his afternoon tea on their best Chinese rug.

Baptizing their babies, marrying their children, burying their dead, he became the personification of the great moments in thousands of lives—a pastor beloved for his patience and understanding.

He could, however, be a formidable enemy for any fool who threatened to undermine the kingdom he had created for himself. His enemies never understood his weapons. Old Fred Johnson never suspected the gentle Andrew would become enraged because his salary was relegated to the least important of the church's expenses. And Fred, the pompous, must have been shocked to find himself being run from the stewards' meeting with one of the parson's fists at the back of his neck and the other at the seat of his pants. Fred, physically excommunicated, never darkened the church door again.

If the town were seething in a moral conflict, Boa became the spearhead for what he believed was right. When it came to alcohol, dry was right. Again the old ladies were taken from their beds and conveyed in the Chrysler Royal to the Town Hall to place their dry vote. As they tottered to put their "X" in the right space, the Reverend laughed and told his best stories to the wets who dared not vent their spleen on a clergyman.

Long was the journey from the solitary youth in the woods, to the beloved pastor in the pulpit. On a June Sabbath morning, he stood at the height of his happiness for his farewell service with his Forest congregation. The orioles warbled in the maples just outside the open windows and the sunbeams cast tiny crosses on the cascades of peonies on the altar. The pews overflowed onto chairs in the aisles; the balcony and the wings were packed. Gripping his left lapel with his left hand, he stood tall, leading the congregation in his rich baritone:

"These things shall be a loftier race,
Than the world hath known shall rise."

VI

Sometimes the deep pathos of human nature, the sublime mystery of the commonplace is clear to us only in retrospect. Andrew Boa was father to me, but the secret river of his being remains veiled in Scottish mists. Rarely did it bubble to the surface. And yet, I have heard its silence.

In childhood, I listened to it daily. His dahlias, his gladioli and I blossomed in the stillness of his patience and love. With him, I weeded, and read, and dreamed my dreams, scarcely knowing where the world of the flower ended and the world of the mortal began.

Gradually forced from my Garden of Eden, confounded by the conflicts of mundane reality, I rarely heard his silence. Sometimes tiptoeing past his room at night, I would see him kneeling by his bed in his trapdoor underwear, and I would tiptoe even more stealthily. Soon I would hear him reading aloud his Bobbie Burns.

Often my mother and I would smile a secret smile when the incessant squeak-squawking of his rocking chair became louder than usual as he studied his Sunday sermon. Involved in our Saturday world of cleaning, buying and baking, we were inclined to forget that a different reality lived on the other side of that study door. When he emerged, he confronted that practical world with a stubborn passive resistance, a sharp whetstone for my mother's earthy Irish temper. Her anger was not mitigated as he exactly tuned the radio for a baseball game or settled himself into his Lazy Boy to watch "Rocket" Richard streak down the ice.

Sometimes he caught us unawares. His river gushed into a whirlpool, and a story surprisingly undignified would rush from his lips, burbling with demonic glee, crafty enough to conceal his own craftiness. His first encounter with my parents-in-law seemed gentle enough until he lifted his eyebrows, pushed back his plate, and began.

"You know, I remember at home when my mother decided the kitchen was too old-fashioned and too hot. We decided to build a summer kitchen where she could cook and we could all eat in the cool of a summer's evening. It was just the time outhouses were going out of style, and so we built our toilet in the house. So you see, where before we went out to shit and came in to eat, we now went out to eat, and came in to shit."

Some demon and some god inhabited that river. Perhaps they warred more fiercely than his calm countenance suggested. One day after I returned from my first year in England, I was dancing in the dining room to my Scottish reel records. Dancing was forbidden in the parsonage, but Father was asleep on the couch in the living room. I was dancing as quickly as I could. Suddenly, he sat bolt upright.

"If you cannot toe properly, Marion, do not dance at all."

"Where did that come from?" I asked utterly astounded. I had heard the anguish in the voice coming from the other side of Damascus.

"Never mind," he said, and returned to his sleeping.

But when I wrote to his sister, my aunt, I discovered that Andy had won all the gold medals for Scottish dancing in Huron County by the age of twenty-five.

The god of that river was a strong god. When village gossips taunted my mother for leaving my father alone sometimes, she laughed and knew she was secure in her laughter.

"Never worry yourself, Mrs. Campbell," she said. "I married the rock of Gibraltar."

And he was that to me for different reasons. In the shifting, uncertain days of university, his weekly epistle always arrived, always containing some parable. I still like best the Greek helmsman who cried out in the hurricane, "Give me the strength to hold the rudder true." The helmsman, the tenacity, the hurricane, the panic and the prayer are magnificently tumbled together in my imagination.

In joy I heard his silence. Gently I had persuaded him to perform my marriage ceremony. Reluctantly he had agreed. Gently I had persuaded him to allow my husband and I to repeat our oaths from memory. Reluctantly he had agreed. But when it came to blessing the rings, that was Anglican stuff without precedent in the United Church. Definitely not! I knew I had struck rock. Then in the middle of the night before our rehearsal, he tapped on my door. He stood there beaming.

"I have found a precedent, Marion, here in this old Scottish psalter. I will type the service on a Christmas calendar and staple it into your wedding book. We will have the blessing of the rings."

In grief, I heard his silence. One Christmas, his best-loved brother Paul was killed in a forest accident. Father disappeared from us for three days. And when he returned, he sat peacefully during a whole evening hanging icicles long and loose on our Christmas tree. And there was another Christmas Eve, when he returned empty-handed from the door after the postman's final round. Crushed with grief, he took the icicles in his great hand and tenderly twined them one by one on the delicate branches.

VII

A single track winds through the Honeyland Swamp. The track of the hound lapping and double-lapping over the retracing of the canny fox flashes upon the inward eye of the hunter. His shoulder aches for the lost burden of his gun. Swirling through his memory like the snowflakes swirling before his eyes are the thoughts that lie too deep for tears—each perfect as a single flake, each lost in the veils of the storm. He trudges on seeking the exact cedar for his grandchild's Christmas tree—yet scarcely seeks at all. Momentarily free of the burden the city forced upon him, his spirit roars its fury in the howl of the north wind, and sings its joy in the freedom of the pathless wood. And the hunter, shrouded in his Gaelic mists, rests on a hollow log, his great shoulders bent towards his knees. Did he take the wrong path? Was there a right path after all?

Suddenly he rises up. With longing eyes, he looks unto the hills. Above the blast of the storm, he cries out, "Lord, I have fought a good fight, I have finished my course, I have kept the faith."

Re-inventing the Archives

Elisavietta Ritchie

Surrounded by flounder, my father and I kneel on a pier. Fish scales in our hair catch the first rays of sunset. We're sunburned, salty and freckled after all day in an open boat. I hauled in my own catch, both hooks full at a time. Both keepers.

I am six. My father is—? Everyone old as parents is old. Only he doesn't seem old. Grownups bend down to tell me how handsome and charming he is, his light English accent melodic, and moustaches are so European—in airports strangers mistake him for Erroll Flynn or Douglas Fairbanks Jr. Brought up to kiss ladies' hands, he still does, even here on Nantucket Island.

How many women has he already loved?

At six, I think only how will we clean all these platter-shaped fish whose eyes migrated topside. My father takes a thin knife, slits bellies, dumps guts over the pier for minnows darting like bees. Then he teaches me to filet: grip the neck of the tail, slice terribly close to the bone.

. . . .

He tells me, years later, of his affairs, even while records spin gypsy guitars and in the next room my mother dumbfounds us by dying.

I grew up to love many men. Does he ever wonder about this part of my life?

. . . .

Anyone who strolls down a fishing pier takes a chance on seeing dead fish, severed heads gulping unfamiliar air, marble eyes unblinking. Not the same as unwrapping Captain Somebody's Fish Sticks Boned and Breaded and Frozen and smothering them with ketchup and tartar sauce so they don't taste of anything that ever swam a sea. Eviscerated fish may be a real turn-off. But if you grow up with them as a matter of course, like the hangman's child—

I've learned: if you are an interested woman, you take your chances with a man like Daddy. You take your chances loving a man who also loves his family, a man curious to learn about everything and about everyone else, whose house is always open to his friends. And to strangers in their need. As in his favorite old Russian song from the Caucasus: *Each guest is sent to us by God / No matter how torn his shirt.*

God was generous. I grew up in a full house.

My father's full and generous life began with his parents. Every evening my Russian grandmother—Babushka—read to the children from Russian, French or English classics. Interesting guests came for tea: they might stay a month.

My Russian grandfather was, people said, a walking encyclopedia. In 1896, while serving as Russia's military attache in Abyssinia, he explored the sources of the White Nile and wrote a book about it. At forty, during the Russo-Japanese war, he became the youngest officer in the Imperial Russian Army to make general. In 1905, he briefly visited America, for the signing of the Peace of Portsmouth, New Hampshire. In August 1914, he refused to sacrifice his troops to the Germans in the battle of Tannenberg. For this, he was courtmartialed, but exonerated, and appointed governor-general of Galicia. Then came the Russian Revolution and continuing civil war, imprisonment, famines, destruction of the old world order.

Russian children grew up with history happening all around them, and at the mercy of others' historical actions. By sixteen and seventeen, my father and my uncle were fighting in the trenches. Both distinguished themselves in action, but Uncle Ivan was killed. A bullet also went through my father's leg, though he survived wounds and illness to escape to America where, on his own at age eighteen, he began a new life. Their parents and sister remained in St. Petersburg/Petrograd/Leningrad.

Most relatives and friends disappeared, were arrested or killed. Between the First World War and the Second, however, a few escaped to Europe. As the Nazis retreated and the Red Army advanced during 1944–1945, my father, this time serving in the American Army, located cousins in various refugee camps. He helped them establish themselves too in the New World.

What stories he tells! I grew up wishing I had more of my own. I envied my father's and grandfather's encyclopedic minds, especially when stumped, as I was when my daughter, then age four, asked me: "Did God make dinosaurs?"

"Presumably," I hedged.

"And who made God?" And, she may later have inquired, what does God want of us? Thinking now of my father, I would answer: To study in depth and width, to put one's energies and knowledge to good uses, to live life to the full.

And Daddy is more energetic, more fun, than anyone I've met. He can swim a river and hike a mountain before breakfast, work all day, sing and dance all night. He often quoted Alfred de Vigny: "One must live in the flames."

He has. That is, when he was younger. Healthier. Before tools began to slip from his trembling fingers, before he misplaced bills and keys and names, before a stroll to the mailbox exhausted him. Still, he talks of joining me for tennis—

So far, after each crisis, he has come back, if never quite as far as before. Terrible, the decline into pain, the side effects of pain-dullers, the indignities of flowered gowns that open behind and strangers who demand, "Ain't he done yet with that bedpan?" Or are late bringing it. And all those friends—where are they now?

So enjoy life while you can. Drain the glass with the old Russian toast, "Drink to the bottom!"

He toasted pinching bottoms too, a popular goal in those days. Nowadays, a woman might scream "Harassment!" and rap more than his knuckles. Yet I wonder how many women, in those days, took overt offense to his advances, though they may have flirted only to a certain point, or laughed at him—more likely with him. I recall giggles.

Even in the nursing home, Daddy flirts. The nurses smile professional smiles. Some flirt back. "Honey, it shows he's alive!"

Surprising women have responded. Surprising to me.

When I was thirteen, while we were standing in the surf fishing, I remarked how ridiculous one of my parents' guests was to swim in a long-sleeved blouse and wide straw hat, "just because she's a redhead, so vain about preserving her fragile death-white skin from freckles."

He glanced at me with amusement. Years later, when he considered me grown up, he confided, "She was an admiral's widow. Also, my mistress."

And once when we were driving past the house of a certain exiled prince, recently deceased, he sighed, "Ah, he was a great friend...We shared the same mistress."

Such revelations emerged accidentally. Perhaps not unwillingly? No malevolence, even unwitting, in his mentioning his adventures to me. Not a devious bone in his body. And he sounded wistful, not boastful.

One long-time suitor still tries—in vain—to seduce me with blow-by-blow accounts of his previous conquests. More than one writer friend informs everyone of his own massive and marvelous exploits in non-literary arenas.

I cannot imagine my father regaling friends—or my mother—with his exploits.

· · · · · · · ·

Suddenly I am aware of the rooster on the adjoining farm. No symbolic cock, this one crows all day long. Exuberantly.

In a pewter goblet on my sill, three marigolds glow like miniature suns, as brash in their brilliance.

· · · · · · · ·

Perhaps I was proud to be accepted as his confidante, although the word conjures up grand opera. Have I seen enough operas and films, read enough books, most of all listened to enough confidences from other men, and from bitter women, to consider Daddy's activities not unusual? At least for men.

Yet he did not lump all women together. Surely he cherished each of his friends for herself—Surely he did not hurt any feelings, or cause problems with their past, present or future husbands—

He was European, gallant, discreet.

Nor, he insists, did he love my mother any less.

. . . .

Well before they met, my mother had shed Kansas City for a more interesting New England and an exotic Paris where, in the mid-1920s, she had met several dashing Russian emigres. Although when my father arrived at Ellis Island, he spoke the King's English and was bent on becoming thoroughly American, she trotted out her few Russian phrases, played Rachmaninoff on the piano for him, and soon Russian hospitality filled their house.

From age three I passed around zakuski: canapés of caviar, smoked eel on grainy black bread, herring in sour cream eaten with miniature silver forks. Thimbles of vodka washed everything down. At dinner, wine.

"And when you open a bottle," Daddy often said, "you toss the cork away."

I've never seen him drunk.

Supposedly tucked into bed hours before, in fact I often fell asleep curled in the tabby's basket outside the dining room where, especially if a guitar or balalaika appeared, songs might continue until dawn.

However haphazardly, my own children have imbibed an eclectic love of music, some interest in their heritage, a penchant for fishy horsd'oeuvres.

. . . .

One morning my daughter comes upstairs from her basement apartment to borrow two eggs. To feed her new lover. Breakfast materializes upstairs, while my father explains to her lover, and to mine, the symbolism of eggs. "Fertility, hope and perfection... Like the egg-shaped domes of Russian churches... The Holy Trinity rolled into one."

He expands and expounds. My mind also wanders... What if, when the bells ring so hard at midnight on Easter, gold cupolas hatched into mystical roosters?

My father, now ill and en route to that perfect elliptical void, has trouble spooning his morning egg. Yet how much he could tell us of the liquid ovoid of loving, fragile shells...

During afternoon visiting hours the nursing home allows "residents" a thimbleful of liquor, though lately even sweet sherry is too strong for my father. He can no longer chew the grainy black bread I used to bring. Or any bread. Caviar is too salty. Smoked eel would choke in his throat. I hold a plastic cup of prune juice to his lips, and sing old Russian marching songs which were my lullabies long ago.

· · · · · · · ·

Mine was a good childhood. My parents shared many friends, many interests from world affairs discussions to weekend excursions into any available countryside, to sculpting statues and playing tennis. They moved often, always creating a garden even from deserts. Everywhere they planted marigolds. How they danced to ragtime, jazz, swing, Gypsy bands! She chided him for dozing through Debussy.

He can catnap anywhere. At the dinner table his super-high energy level may suddenly drop, in mid-sentence his eyes close. He remains bolt upright, and after five minutes' respite resumes the conversation without losing a beat. This also happens to me.

Although after marriage my mother gave up the piano—"If there isn't time to practice Beethoven and Chopin six hours a day, there's no point in dabbling"—she soon had other careers, at a time few women did. Daddy was proud of her. Increasingly in later years he hated to be without her, continued to hug her, and pinch her bottom. Obvious to everyone that he loved her deeply.

"Your mother was a very sexy girl," he told me.

I wonder now: How did my mother feel about his philandering? I wonder if or how much she knew. Was she, who usually believed the best about everyone, naive? She may have continued to love and put up with him (I think forgive-and-forget in these matters is a myth) because he was dazzling and thoughtful and delightful. Did she take as a compliment the fact that other women also found him extraordinarily attractive?

Beethoven on my radio, the rooster crowing beyond the hedge.

As a child I sometimes worried that their marriage, like that of one schoolmate's parents, might break up. Divorces were rare events, scandalous. One day I ran up to my mother urgently. "Mummy! Daddy is flirting with that lady again! Are you going to divorce him?"

"Oh, no, darling," she laughed. "He isn't serious. And no one takes him seriously."

Still, my parents' marriage was a good one, I think... My mother may have a different side to the story. Someday I should tackle that theme. Even face how her history affects mine.

Too late.

· · · · · · · ·

Let us consider some hypotheses.

Perhaps my mother drank because he strayed.

Perhaps he strayed because she drank.

More likely, circumstances played the major role, and opportunities. My father frequently had to travel abroad, sometimes for long periods. As he pointed out in some history lesson to me, once a Roman soldier crossed three rivers, whatever he did was no longer considered infidelity. (Whatever the soldier's house-bound, hut-bound, wife could do was apparently not up for consideration.)

Early in World War Two, a war during which, by then a major in the American Army, he was again to distinguish himself on several battlefields, my father was stationed in North Africa. Although his V-letters home spoke of his "old Arab housekeeper," years later a snapshot of a beautiful dark young woman slipped from a book and he told me of that long-ago adventure.

Though the housekeeper surely found new employers and new loves when Daddy traveled on, she kept his pallid legacy, embarrassing or cherished gift, to term. My bastard half-sister may still survive beneath the palms of Marrakesh.

When after four years Daddy came marching home, a silver eagle on his shoulder, did he look past me to imagine that distant, other, smaller, daughter? Did he wonder if she also inherited sapphire eyes, freckles, carrot hair? Or did she—does she—resemble her dusky mother?

· · · · · · · ·

A passion for acquiring and sharing knowledge in any field, especially history, included a love for reciting poetry. From his childhood, Russian folk ballads. From his years in the Orient, Rudyard Kipling's "Gunga Din," "The captain's lady and Lily O'Grady are sisters under the skin" and "I've taken my fun where I've found it." After his first trip to Alaska, Robert W. Service, beginning with "The Shooting of Dan McGrew."

Across the dinner table, like courting Malayans exchanging couplets of pantuns, my father and I rattle off verse after verse, from "A bunch of the boys were whooping it up in the Malamute Saloon—" through the fatal encounter between Dangerous Dan McGrew and The Lady That's Known as Lou.

Or we launch into "The Cremation of Sam McGee."
There are strange things done in the midnight sun
By the men who moil for gold;
The Arctic trails have their secret tales
That would make your blood run cold;

The Northern Lights have seen queer sights,
But the queerest they ever did see
Was the night on the marge of Lake Lebarge
I cremated Sam McGee.

And on through one hundred twenty lines of the narrator's misadventures with his "frozen chum," Sam McGee from Tennessee, until discovering the perfect "cre-ma-to-ri-um."

"That's not poetry!" my mother would scold, slurring words. She loved Keats, Byron, Spenser, Wordsworth, Longfellow, Milton. During her year in France, she studied Racine, Lamartine, Valéry.

Without missing a stride, Daddy would launch into Service's "Madame La Marquise," about a snowy-haired aristocrat married to the Marquis de la Glaciere, her counterpart in rectitude and haughtiness. One day their son knocked at his father's study:

Said Hongre de la Glacière unto his proud papa,
"I want to take a wife, mon père." The marquis laughed, "Ha ha,
And whose, my son?" he slyly said, but Hongre with a frown
Cried "Fi, Papa, I mean to wed, I want to settle down!"

Hongre reveals the name: Raymonde de la Veale.
What made the Marquis start and stare and clutch his perfumed beard?
What made him stagger to a chair and murmur, "As I feared....
Her mother was your mother's friend and we were much together.
Ah, well, you know how such things end: I blame it on the weather.
We had a very sultry spell… You cannot wed Raymonde, my boy, because
I am her father."

Hongre is devastated, but in a few years returns with the name of Mirabelle du Veau.

She too proves to be Hongre's sister. Grief-stricken again, he rushes from his papa's study. This time his seemingly rigid and frigid mother intercepts him.

"What ails you so, my darling boy? What throngs of sorrow spite you?...Come, tell me, I invite you."

"If I told you, Mother dear....Another's honour would, I fear, be in the soup forever."

Finally he blurts out his despair. But Madame La Marquise is strangely unperturbed.

"You can wed Mirabelle, my boy, Or Raymonde if you'd rather
For I as well the truth may tell: Papa is not your father."

Suddenly now, with the twilight crowing of the cock, I wonder if, in all that, Daddy had a message for me....

. . . .

Today a postcard arrived from the Arctic, from a new friend. He has told me he was adopted at birth and remains ignorant of his parents, but recently began inquiries.

The postcard shows a trio of polar bears. The mother, dark-muzzled, leads two cubs over the floes. Her feet stand square on one raft of ice. The camera caught the first cub in his mother's wake, front paws on her float, his black nose close behind her white tail, like Babar's procession of elephants. His hind feet stretch from the floe where his twin stares toward the lens as if, when he's grown, he would eat it. The first cub is about to fall, belly-flop into the drink.

Islets of ice drift into polar infinity. Floes shift like lily pads in a summer pond under the hopscotch of frogs.

Did my friend choose this card half-aware of an innate longing for family? The perils of separation? Did he guess that I, like the mother bear, still try to guide my progeny through dangerous passages, since the world, even in our temperate zone, can be slippery, cold.

I picture my friend trudging across urban snow into a brick municipal hall. He seeks a sign: ORIGINS INFORMATION CENTRE. Day after day, he waits in line, while snowy boots puddle into dark seas, questions leave more question marks. Like navigating through Arctic straits: icebergs surround, blizzards engulf, what one hoped was safe harbour proves to be icebound.

Children (inevitably) irked with imperfect parents often imagine:

I was adopted, my real dad is the Storm King, my mother—the Snow Queen.

Yet we are all scions of princes raised by the shepherd's wife. Locked in the vault, our crowns await us. Minions will rush out with roses to greet us. Our kingdoms stretch rich and green. Meanwhile, we tend royal sheep, whiter, more woolly, than polar bears.

. . . .

No doubt about my own origins. "You, child, inherited all our faults and none of our virtues," my parents would sometimes tease. "Though neither of us has eyes that gleam in the dark, like a fox caught in headlight beams." So I don't think my true father was a sharecropper from Tennessee, or a French count with a penchant for innocent American schoolgirls like my mother.

Do my eyes still gleam in the dark?

. . . .

I don't remember my parents undertaking those classic lectures on the Facts of Life, though when I was eight my mother left out a book with black-and-white photos of dogs and flowers, the text only hinting how they do it.

. . . .

One day when my daughter was fifteen we were sitting on the porch with two of her classmates, shelling peas and stringing beans while monsoon rains turned the screens into curtains. Meanwhile we discussed The

IUD versus The Pill, subjects suddenly in the news but not yet dinner-table conversation in front of children, especially other people's. But this seemed a rare opportunity to bring up a subject I'd avoided.

"If by chance you were to get knocked up," I told my daughter in the presence of her friends, "of course you should have it, like an appendix, out…. Still, if the father were brilliant and wonderful, yet you were too young to marry—and why ruin two future careers—then you could quietly have the child—and I'd raise it, pass it off as my own. No point in wasting good genes."

This hasn't happened yet. Now she rather wishes it would.

· · · · · · · ·

In later years my father told me that my mother had been pregnant several times, while married, first when they were newlywed in the Philippines and traveling too much, and later, in Chicago during the Depression, they "couldn't afford more than one."

Strange spin of the genetic roulette wheel that I should be the only one spared…in this hemisphere.

While loving and super-conscientious, my mother dreaded becoming a "brood mare and mere housewife." Her salary—albeit of course half my father's—paid a housekeeper to look after me as well as my father's mother, who at last escaped from Leningrad and lived with us, and my American grandmother who frequently visited from Kansas City. So I was an only child raised by at least four women and one man. (When my turn came, domestics were too expensive, my mother and mother-in-law drank too much to entrust either with baby-sitting, and I bore not one but three children.)

Yet my father loved children, claimed to want eight, at least so that each could follow one of the careers he wished for himself—doctor, scientist, sculptor, general, explorer, agronomist, historian, and inventor of gadgets to advance humanity and enrich everyone.

I realize this instant: I must still be struggling to fulfill the appointed roles of all his other, unborn, children. In vain, of course, and not only as a girl unable to carry on his distinguished unpronounceable family name, or do the math necessary to enter the sciences. Still, writing is a way for a solitary to live vicariously.

And some nights this house resounds with my invisible siblings. I cannot see their faces, but their blue eyes shine in the dark. I know each also bears our father's nose, our wide cheekbones and jaws, freckles. I hear them whispering up in the eaves, exchanging the dates of battles and the solutions to insoluble equations, arguing the merits of Rodin versus Claudel, or the benefits of no-till sowing of soybeans in the old corn field, or describing—their unseen hands defining circles—the workings of some amazing apparatus they're creating. All in a babel of tongues to flesh out his dreams.

. . . .

And you, my sister off in Marrakesh, are you leading revolutions, or a herd of donkeys to the waterhole?

. . . .

The neighbor's rooster grows silent with twilight. Time to light a candle.

. . . .

At the end of the pier my daughter, then aged three, baited all three hooks herself, the first with a clam neck, the second with a bloodworm, the third with a slice of spot. My father watched her cast the line into the cove, then reel in her line.

"Look, Grandfather!" she shouted, almost falling into the water. "A fish bit every hook!"

Silvery perch, too small to keep.

"Best let them grow up. Here, let me show you how to extract the hooks without injuring the mouths."

Was it my father, or I, who taught her to clean the bigger fish of later years? No matter, she learned, and to poach them in wine.

And, as if to please her grandfather and me, though she would have done so anyway, she has become a doctor, a scientist, writer, and soldier. In the front lines too. How proud Daddy would be to see me pin a maple leaf on her shoulder. She hurries home from the hospital to dig in her garden and write a poem while the bread she sculpted for old friends and new suitors bakes in the oven, and they will sing and dance all night, and in the morning, scale a literal cliff, explore a real cave.

· · · · · · · ·

My own life remains full. The men who most fascinate me are brilliant discoursers on many topics, generous adventurers with boundless energies, men of immense—ego? Or merely joie de vivre? Foreigners, mostly, often from the eastern reaches of Europe, they have suffered the consequences of other people's wars, and fought in them, either in somebody's army, or as partisans against somebody's army. They have loved their wives, and other women as well. For them, I was only one in their long line, and I knew it. Each of them was only one in my somewhat shorter line, and mostly they did not know it.

Let the roosters crow all they want.

· · · · · · · ·

Toward the end of her life, my father seemed wholly and solely content with my mother. So I, at some midpoint now, find myself filled by loving one man. A brilliant, generous adventurer, half-European, one who has also loved widely, and had to fight in a war.

· · · · · · · ·

On alternate days my stepmother and I drive to the nursing home. We sit beside my father's narrow cranked-up bed, trying to decipher his disconnected whispers, trying to persuade him to eat, trying to persuade nurses and orderlies to tend him more quickly. Occasionally I end up doing basic procedures like changing and cleaning him up myself. My stepmother draws the line at feeding. That is, understandably, why she, a saint but also increasingly frail, couldn't keep him at home any longer.

Though his hearing aid disappeared in the institutional laundry, to pass the time, because he seems to enjoy it, I read aloud from the newspaper. Or I recite what I can remember from Rudyard Kipling, though he is now "politically incorrect," or from Robert W. Service, though my mother was correct: as poetry his is, at best, dated.

Our words are anyway drowned by loudspeakers and televisions everywhere, other patients crying "Nurse, nurse, help me! Nurse!" My compassionate Daddy, who used to ring for a nurse to go help them, can no longer work the bell, or no longer hears their plaints.

"He only thinks of himself now," my stepmother sighs.

"At his age, ma'am," the nurse answers, "that's normal."

It is not normal that in four months he's lost fifteen pounds. The staff explains that, despite their sweet talk, he refuses food. Still, with my urging, he will open his clenched lips for a thimbleful of juice or yogurt.

"And when I stopped at the nursing home today," I am able to report to my stepmother, "Daddy ate four spoonfuls of strawberry ice cream. Then he actually spoke, said something like 'One must live—.' As I was feeding him, the doctor stopped in, and insisted the only way for Daddy to get proper nourishment is to transfer him to the hospital where they can feed him intravenously. The doctor and I arranged for a bed tomorrow—"

My stepmother is aghast. "But we agreed—No heroic measures—"

"Nothing 'heroic' about—One can't let a person die of mere dehydration, malnutrition, just because the nursing home can't insert IVs."

"I thought I was handling these matters...I am his wife."

"Yes, yes, of course, and you're a saint, it's just that—"

I have overstepped my role. But I happened to be there when the doctor—

. . . .

My father knows when I'm there. His hands gripping mine are surprisingly strong. He is not ready to die.

I'm not ready to let him. However tenuous, skeletal, we remain flesh and blood.

And, unconsciously, I seem to have forgiven my father everything without my blinkered mind ever before having raised the question of anything to forgive. Have I become, unwittingly and long after the fact, not just confidante but accomplice to that old-fashioned double standard?

· · · · · · · ·

Midnight. The breeze through the dark window rises, but the three marigolds in the pewter goblet remain unruffled, stiff. I must remember to take them to the nursing home tomorrow.

The candle flame writhes in the wind. I place the hurricane globe, a tall bulging glass sheath, over the candlestick. The flame now stays vertical, steady.

Then I put the base of the pewter goblet holding the marigolds over the narrow top of the hurricane glass. Inside, the candle still burns brightly. Must be crazy, that old law of physics about vacuums extinguishing fires.

Gradually the goblet's base grows too hot to touch. Only a blue flicker on the wick remains. The room dims. I remove the goblet. With the inflow of air, the flame flares, rekindles the room. I cover the candle again. Again the fire trapped within the glass dies down. Then—Abracadabra!—at the final instant, I remove the chalice, the flame flares high.

Then I remember that pewter melts. Time to give up playing. It's late.

The candle will not snuff. So I blow, three, four times. Finally with the fifth strong puff the flame bends, bows out. Inside the globe, the thread of smoke winds and winds.

War-Gone

C.B. Follett

I was not seasoned by my father,
who went to war unbidden,
and reckless, flowed a blood river.
I wanted to tear his star-eyes,
rip him from my mother's tears,
shake him off over the compost heap,
and bid the worms consume
his betrayal of me.

The Worst Business

· ·

Peter Such

Until Grandad oiled its hinges, the Pearly Gates wouldn't swing open. Not that it mattered, but he was a perfectionist. His soldered wire creation finally finished, he leaned back to admire it, squinting his right eye against smoke rising from the fag-end of an Old Woodbine stuck to his lip and in imminent danger of burning it. Just as I thought to myself, *He's forgot it this time*, out flips his tongue like a lizard and—bob's your uncle—he scoops the hot coal right into his mouth. By day's end he'd have thirty or forty in there, a mushy wad of nicotine in his cheek. "'elps soothe this bleedin' toothache," he'd say.

"You should have that lot took out," Granny would mutter.

In those days, you paid for dentists; so, soon as there was trouble, you had them all out, like tonsils and appendixes, the sooner in life the better. I wasn't looking forward to it.

From the cobble-floored storage cellar, I'd already helped lug in damp redolent sacks filled with compressed moss. Grandma cut the strings around their collars. I began ripping out moist handfuls and piling them beside her on a wooden bench. Its top was covered with lino faded brown except at the borders where yellow and green flowers still bloomed. Gran had painted them on when they first got the flower shop. They were a happy pair back then, picked for Pearly King and Queen. This ritual had nothing to do with the Pearly Gates, it had been explained to me.

Granny began wiring clumps of moss to Grandad's framework, in this instance the top-of-the-line funeral choice, four feet high, with steps going up and down to the arched gates crowned with angels' wings. Gradually Grandad's armature began to take on solid green shape. Over Grandad's bones went Granny's flesh.

This was the secret of their time together, wasn't it? He: sharp, spiffy, quick-witted, quick-footed, quick-fisted—a jaunty bantam with his cap over one eye, ready to take on the biggest stevedore if necessary. And she: earthy yet dreamy, practical yet artistic, capable of the most outlandish outrage and the most outlandish love. Most of all, though, she was that haven, where, though I never saw it, Grandad could softly crumple down, those times when his cocky spirit was deeply broken.

A big funeral order like this was going to take all night. As part of my apprenticeship, I was allowed to moss up the many simply-shaped wire wreaths that would lie with the Pearly Gates on top of the coffin as it wended its way into the cemetery. You had to make sure the moss was neither too compressed nor left too loose. Either way, Gran cut the wire and I'd have to do it again.

Funeral orders put everyone on edge. It was bad enough managing the regular day-to-day business of a rented flowershop. "Didn't 'ave to get all airyated wiv bleedin' funeral orders when I 'ad nofink but me old barra ter push," Grandad would say.

And he had a case there. A barrow you owned, not rented. And closing time was any time. In 1947, we didn't have fridge-cases like the new big florist's chains. For us, the flower trade was a matter of life and death. Sometimes you could watch helplessly as the morning's unsold stock gradually died off despite fresh water and ground-up aspirins. Every dead blossom at the day's end was a betrayal, and a bad smell at the bottom of a large blue vase sometimes meant a week's rent for the store.

For funerals, Grandad had to make a special trip to Covent Garden market. That meant being bright and alert at three-thirty a.m. to haggle with traders so sharp, as Grandad put it, that one day they'd cut themselves. Unlike weddings, or decorating synagogues, funeral planning was not exactly long-range. You had to make do with whatever you could find in the cutthroat old market stalls at the time. Do you pay full price for what you really want, or wait 'til five to get it cheaper, maybe losing it all together?

Hinging on one or two gambles like that was your whole profit margin.

Exciting though. For one thing, if it was an all-nighter, then I got to get out of school the next day. And look at all the extra dosh we might make. Sometimes, as Grandad put it, since your flowers didn't have to last beyond the grave, you could afford to buy marginal stock, cheat the devil, and make a killing. In fact it was almost as good as what you could do by "finding the rightful owners" of commodities which "fell from the back of a lorry" on their way from the Bermondsey docks. (An amazingly frequent event, which resulted in a certain secret cupboard in Granny's house which looked like the wallpapered panels on the rest of the wall being mysteriously replenished with one hundred boxes of chocolates one week, twenty huge cans of corned beef stamped *London Rifle Brigade* the next, and several fur coats at Christmas time.)

By the time all the mossing up was done, it was past midnight. It was a bleeder of a winter night out, wet with sleet. Grandad took me out with him to see if we could warm Alf up. Usually this took about fifteen minutes of exertion, the only time Grandad didn't smoke. By now, I'd been erratically trained into the mysteries of the degree of choke, amount of throttle and retard of spark so that when Grandad would swing the long cranking handle to make Alf's engine burp and bobble, I had some skill in "keepin' 'er goin'." Nothing in the world could match our triumph at hearing the 28 Wolseley's whimsical motor, which had never known the luxury of an electric starter, burst into full-bodied, all-six-cylinders life.

But tonight was not the night. Grandad's exertions shook the hearse-like old body on its springs, but to no avail. Only once did the heart leap as two cylinders fired, but the result was a backfire that sent the handle viciously twisting backwards, bruising Grandad's wrist. He went in to get sympathy and an Old Woodbine.

"That'll teach yer ter respect the dead," Gran muttered.

"Better 'im being bleedin' dead than Alf. 'Ow you fink me an' the nipper's goin' ter git yer bleedin' flowers then? Answer me that one."

"You'll make Alf go. You always do."

"There's always a bleedin' first time," he finished cynically, proud, nevertheless, of her confidence in him.

"How's about a spot of tea?" I said.

"That's it, son," Grandad said.

While I put on the kettle, out he went. By the time tea was made he'd returned with the spark plugs and sat "gingering" them with a piece of sandpaper. Once they were cleaned and the gap measured with his thumbnail, Grandad popped them into the oven of our old black stove. Since it was so rarely used, I recognized this as a draconian measure.

After fortifying himself with a cup of tea and another Old Woodbine, Grandad went out to try Alf again, carrying the hot spark plugs wrapped in rags. I was keen to go out and help him, but Gran had noticed me looking puffy-eyed. Since the school authorities had been making noises about my occasional absences and about how anaemic I looked, Gran was worried one of those snotty social workers might come round again and have me dumped into an orphanage. So she was all for having me take a little kip, in case Grandad would need me later on to go to Covent Garden.

I curled into the musty upholstery of the broken-backed couch, twining myself strategically around a popped-up spring, cuddling my favorite pillow. Grandma sat on the arm, tucking me in under a thick comforter she'd inherited from her Granny, the one who was a Gypsy, or so she said. With the smoke from her cigarette curling up into the golden halo of weak light, she did indeed look dark and mysterious. I thought of the gyppos I'd run into down in Kent when we went hop-picking. One little girl my age sat beside me round the campfire, singing along, always smiling, until her mother found her and dragged her off. By then I was in love with her. Now I thought I knew why.

I studied Gran's face as she sat taking a break while she settled me. I felt that aura about her of people who, all of their lives, don't ever expect to rest, or ever to be free of those who harass, mock or condemn them; and yet who know they are somehow blessed, because, even when forced into the most humiliating service, remain always free.

Whatever she made was always so rare and beautiful people couldn't get over it. They would thank her, they would bless her, they would cry over her. At that moment, though, I said to myself: *It ain't really them nobs she does it for, is it?* Watching the glinting roundels of her hoop earrings swing soft against her cheek, I knew she had the power of magic. Her mind and hands connected through those flowers to another kind of world as real or realer than this one.

I don't know when the dream started. In it, I went up to the back room overhead, sort of sifting through the ceiling. I could look down and see Granny still sitting there smoking as if from afar. All I know is I was called upon to open that back room's window and I did so. I trod over the sill and placed my feet gingerly down on the corrugated iron of the shed roof below. The second great war was recently ended. Whether, then, my dead father, shot down over the Bay of Biscay trying to rescue the men bobbing helpless in the cruel sea was in this dream I'm not sure.

They were certainly light and heavenly beings who met me there, coming out of the night sky like gliders over the housing estate apartments like people in 3D movies. They put a sword in my hand, and without their saying anything I knew that meant I was doomed forever to fight against unfairness and injustice. "All right," I said. "That's what I'll do, then."

"We ain't expectin' miracles," they said, speaking rather strangely, I thought, in good cockney. "Give it a good go. Be brave and fair, mate. All that sort of thing. Never back down. That goes wivout sayin'. You're a bit of a tich, a nipper like your Grandad; but you're strong. And now and again we'll 'elp yer out if fings gets really devastatin'."

"Thanks. I likes to know there's a few mates on my side."

"Ta ta then!" And the angels were gone.

When I woke it was some time later. There was a great pile of stubbed-up ferns on the table and Gran and Grandad were sitting looking pretty rough.

"'Allo. Young nipper's awake."

"Everything all right?" I asked.

"No. It ain't, mate. 'Ere it is, 'alf past three o' clock, and Alf won't go."

"You tried everyfink?"

"Everyfink. 'E's dead. We better 'old this bleedin' funeral for 'im."

"You'll manage somehow, Ducks. I know you," said Granny.

I saw the panic in his eye, though; and I thought, *Blimey! This ain't fair. This ain't fair at all.*

"The day that van starts will be the day roses grow blue," he said.

"Come on," I said. "You know how sometimes it just floods and all Alf needs is a few minutes to dry out. You should've had me there to keep it goin'. Give it one more go."

"Useless. It's bleedin' useless. 'Specially with this duff wrist."

Still, he followed me out. The sleet had stopped and a muddy light illuminated the far reaches of a scudding grey sky.

"Can't lose nofink trying. Leave the choke right in, Nipper, and open the throttle."

I did as he said. Grandad turned the starting handle round to the engine's compression point, then swung it down hard. Alf spluttered, coughed, bobbled... died.

"Almost went that time, Grandad."

He made no reply. The effort, coming on top of the two futile hours he'd already spent, had cost him dearly. He sucked in air, then began coughing vigorously. After a few more wheezes, his tubes seemed cleared and he gathered himself for another go, first fiddling with the magneto and using his rags to dry off the distributor cap.

"Alright, then. Let's 'ave at yer!"

Down he squatted, braced himself, turned the handle to the cylinder with most compression. It wasn't fair Grandad couldn't afford a car in good nick. It wasn't fair Alf wouldn't go and so many people would be disappointed. In the spellbound quiet of the old wooden van, reeking with the smell of dry rot and ancient leather, I looked up onto the shed roof. I concentrated.

Grandad took in a deep breath and threw his whole body into it.

The engine caught fire with such gusto and suddenness I sat stunned until a faltering note and Grandad's yell to "Keep it goin' Nipper!" got me to put my foot on the accelerator and keep a hand on the choke.

And so we were off, Granny's "order" in hand, so I could read it off to remind Grandad of anything. Past Rotherhythe, we turned onto Tower Bridge.

I always enjoyed going "over the water," because that's where the "Nobs" lived. Not that we ever met, at Covent Garden or anywhere else, except, I later learned, for nefarious reasons. When we were there, they were asleep. And when they were at the opera and gadding about, we were working.

The great slimy river glinted and wobbled between its stony banks like a jellied eel. All along the embankment street lamps glimmered in morning mist, heads stuck on poles, and down towards the Isle of Dogs and Greenwich a line of empty barges thought about the open sea.

We were late at the market, made later by the problem of parking until an old stallmate of Grandad's moved his lorry and we snugged up against a pile of split cane boxes holding mimosa. It was dull and echoing under the damp arcades, dim pools of light barely illuminating the crammed blossoms, hawkers' voices clanging in the vaults above.

I shivered with tiredness as much as with the cold as Grandad did his best to negotiate. It was a big funeral order, not easy to fill. On these occasions, Grandad never bought exactly what was written, even though I was there to read it out to him. He'd never really caught on to "all that alphabet lark" the way Granny had. He had a knack, though, for making substitutions, depending on what he found and at what price, that rarely went against the grain of Granny's design sense.

But today he was floundering. I could sense he was not his usual chipper self, unable to hold his own, for once, with the banter and repartee of the hawkers, hesitating too long at some places, ready to buy but unsure of quality, sure of quality but leery of price. So it went until we had passed some subtle moment and the market was suddenly devoid of everything but secondary stock. We were forced into a quick collecting to fill Granny's order, rushing back to previously haggled-with stall-owners to find the flowers now unavailable, having to take a chance on marginal items.

At the end, though, Grandad thought he'd found some luck. There were several boxes of white roses, not sold because they were at full bloom and not likely to last for more than a day or two if they were to be retailed in bunches. But for the funeral they would just do, and his clever Allie could use the luxury of them in place of the dozen white lilies she'd originally asked for.

The deal was struck and we lugged this last load into the van. Grandad's hand had swollen badly and so I asked him if he would just this once let me try to start Alf up.

"Why not?" he said. "You needs ter learn sometime."

"Grandad," I said, picking up the handle from behind the front seat, "it ain't right the way I see it. You could work in Peak Frean's or Cadbury's Chocolates and make several quid a day. I mean, look at how you and Gran 'ave ter go on. I ask yer."

He looked at me with some kind of shock, which turned into an expression of great soft concern. "'Ere, Son. Look at me."

I did so, letting the starting handle dangle down beside me. He only said that when there was something important he wanted me to know.

"Remember this, Nipper" (putting his hand gently on my shoulder) "and you mark my words for when I'm dead and gone. The worst business, the very worst business, Nipper, is better than the best job. Go on then, start this bleedin' van."

Unbelievably, it roared into life first time. I looked around to see if any of the stallmen had seen my feat. None had; but from that time forward Grandad turned the handle over to me.

Gran had been "all agitated" waiting for our return. Now she burst into action. We started with the simple stuff first: round wreaths and a couple of cushions. She always did this, growing familiar with the stock we'd bought, allowing the decision of what to use to percolate in her mind so that the grand finale, in this case the Pearly Gates, would be the triumphant conclusion to her long night's work.

I was nauseous with the odor of packed blossoms and bitter tea. But I knew I'd soon doss down for a long sleep, excused from school for the coming day. Then it happened.

When Gran came to the white roses and opened the boxes, only the top two were white and unblemished. Some nasty nip in the air where the roses had been stored had begun to brown the others' petals. The stallman had probably not even noticed himself. But there was no turning back. All the other flowers of various kinds and colors had been used. It was these or nothing.

Gran didn't look at us. She stared down at the floor.

I thought, *we can't get out of this one.*

There's only two hours to go before the bloke is put into his scrimp and save. And it don't matter whether the Pearly Gates opens or closes. Going to a funeral in brown boots is bad enough, without you also got brown roses.

I don't know why it came out in poetry like that, but the next thing I knew I was saying it out loud. I thought at first I was going to get a clock on the ear'ole. It was dreadful quiet, and Grandad's face looked black as Newgate's knocker. Then Gran did a snort through her long nose which I wasn't sure was laughing or crying 'til the next one. She hung onto the table to stop from falling down, her face all creased up wiv it. Then Grandad begin to see the funny side of it too, and he spits out his wad of dog-ends into the fireplace so's he can let out the giggle. Soon we was all laughing, all rolling on the floor in a proper cockney schlemozzle, hugging and crying.

"Go on, get the bathtub!" Gran yelled. "I been finking a summink I been wanting to try for years."

So I got the galvanized tub we filled once a week with hot water. Granny stood over it, Gypsy and mysterious, muttering to herself, pouring in cold water and scattering on its surface some powder from a sachet she'd opened, stirring the mix with a wooden spoon. Then she took the roses and cut their stems short on the diagonal, at the length they'd be needed, and set them, heads up, ranged round the tub with their stems in the water.

"Cuppa tea?" Grandad asked.

"Might as well," Gran replied.

"I fink the nipper should turn in. Been a lovely lad you 'as, my son."

I was tired but I didn't want to miss anything. "Cor! That ain't fair."

"Don't you two start," Gran warned. "You shouldn't come the old acid with Grandad now, Nipper. He'll knock you up in time ter see the Pearlies, don't you worry."

"S'truth, ain't it? Your Gran'll fink er summink."

"Oh, alright then."

Well, they did wake me as promised. And the men came in from the undertakers to take the funeral order out to the hearse. And they did the whole thing up with knobs on it. I couldn't help going on after it on my bike, even though I was supposed to be in school.

You'd hardly believe it. "You never see the like!" people exclaimed afterwards. "That Allie is a proper caution, she is. Who'd've thought it up but her, I ask you?"

Gran had managed to dye those roses to hide the brown. They were blue roses. A deep beautiful blue those roses, nestled against fern green all over the Pearly Gates of Heaven. Cor! What a way to go down!

Well, I don't know as how they was looking out for us or not, those angels. They seem to 'ave done me all right in the main since. Anyway, Gran went down in history with that one, snatchin' victory from the jaws of defeat.

As all us types 'ave to do. Just to keep going.

Prayer For My Father

Robert Bly

Your head is still
Restless, rolling
East and west.
That body in you
Insisting on living
Is the old hawk
For whom the world
Darkens.
If I am not
With you when you die,
That is grievous
But just.
That part of you
Cleaned my bones more
Than once. But I
Will meet you
In the young hawk
Whom I see
Inside both
You and me. He
Will guide you
To the Lord of Night,
Who will give you
The tenderness
You wanted here.

A Pot Full of Green Beans

Mike Lipstock

To this day I can't look at a green stringbean without seeing my father bent over an old work table and weeping. It was 1935 and he was a violin teacher who had lost most of his pupils. The depression had eroded his practice and even his old friends... Brahms... Chopin... Beethoven couldn't help him. The slim translucent fingers that created such beautiful music had to find another way to provide a living for his family. But... he was fortunate—those same hands could fix anything. He was a maestro with a hammer and saw as well as a fiddle.

I can still remember that cold winter when I was fourteen. He was making fifteen dollars a week and was worrying himself sick about how he would pay the rent. In those days that was the first priority for every family. Mom had to go back to work and Dorothy my older sister, ready to start college, became a packer at Macy's. The four of us doubled up, and we rented two rooms to a couple of Russians who sold watches from their pushcarts.

Pop and I found a source for discarded lumber. We salvaged scraps from the construction yards and he made small tables and bookcases... the splits and knots were hidden with wide moulding and thick layers of paint. We held garageless garage sales out in the streets before the rest of the world ever heard of them. He sold some, but still, there was not enough money for the four of us to live on. Mama and Dorothy would have to continue working... he grieved for his lost world. From day to day I watched his great courage and fifty years later when my own life was on the line I would close my eyes and see Papa battling for survival.

In desperation he sought out his rich brother, the schoolteacher who

lent him the down payment plus an extra hundred bucks, and Damn! if he
didn't buy a foreclosed shack in upstate New York. Four hundred bucks,
a hundred down, and a couple of rooms... but... it came with three cleared
acres. All of this from a Strout realty catalog.

...Mama asked but one question.

"What do you know about farming?

"Nothing, but I have the whole winter and a library to learn it."

The deed was done and the house was now the repository for every
seed catalog and agricultural booklet printed. He and I scrounged the
pushcarts of Brownsville and Orchard Street for old hoes, picks, axes, and
of course burlap bags to bring back the harvest. Our Russian watchmak-
ers also brought home tools and ideas for the farm. Mama and Dorothy
had no enthusiasm... but to me he was a hero... he was Daniel Boone setting out in the wilderness to build a new life... I worshipped him.

In June when school was finally over we went up to see the three acres.
The Strout man took us up the broken shale road, and a mile before the
house we had to get out and walk. Small trees had sprouted on the unused
road and made it impassable. The small house was old, broken-down and
simply worn out... the three acres of "cleared land" was a mine field strewn
with boulders. The roof leaked, and the outhouse had been home to a family of woodchucks. The water was in a well two hundred feet from the house
and we cooked on an outdoor pit that we made of rocks... But we worked
eighteen hours a day and even started to talk about Mama coming up.

The turning point came when we met Wally Davis, a neighboring dairy
farmer who looked about a hundred. Through the eyes of a fourteen-year-
old, Wally had the same feelings for the land that my father had for a Brahms
violin concerto... He was sympathetic and knew that we were flat broke.
For four bucks he said he would bring over a team of horses, plow up the
rocky acres and show us how to plant. We agreed... and watched in wonder as he cut his furrows straight and released the rich soil from the beds
of rock that held it captive for ages. He cut chunks of eyes from the potatoes and showed Papa just how to plant them... This was to be our bumper
crop. For two weeks we broke our backs getting those potatoes under the

earth... two acres... and another as a garden to live on.

String beans!!! He was crazy about planting them and building trellises to hold them in place. He had visions of radishes, plum tomatoes, vines of cucumber and eggplant. But for now all we had was seed. How would we live? It was then that he sold us to Wally for three bucks apiece a week. We were going to him as mules. To save gas we walked the two miles, and Wally put us out in the fields to load hay that he had cut with his sharp scythe. Clumps of the golden feed lay waiting for our muscles and labor to haul them into the weathered old barn. We tossed the hay with identical left-handed swings. Wally waited on top to pile and store it for winter feed. When you toss for hours you soon forget all about Mozart trios and rotten marks in French. We had six bucks a week coming in and Wally always threw in a dozen eggs and a couple of chickens as a bonus. We worked for him from Monday to Friday but on weekends we worked on the garden. Slowly we could see the green stubble of the potatoes coming up. The stringbeans had tendrils like octopus arms... vines shot out in every direction and it took rolls of twine to tame them. On Sundays Pop took me to the heights of Nirvana. He taught me to drive his 1930 model A Ford... Ah, if my friends could see me now!!!

He never let me share his inner turmoil... a wife and daughter working to pay the rent. That was the disgrace eating away at his soul. We found a pond in the woods and with Wally's hooks and our tree limbs and cord, we dug out worms and caught fish by the dozen. He boiled up a fish stew with stringbeans and anything else he had on hand and I loved it. For me it was the summer of my life. The beans continued to grow and soon we were eating them by the pound. It was then that I found him crying his heart out. We were exhausted after a day in the fields and all that we could scrape together was a pot full of green beans... everything was finally closing in on him... he was crumbling.

"Mikey, we have nothing to eat!!" he cried. "What have I done to you? What have I done to my family?" He wept for a family that he no longer had. He was devastated... Mom had written, heartbroken, and wanted to come up.

Me, the young adolescent, was trying to console him. "What," he asked, "will she eat? Fish and string beans? The place isn't ready, we have no gas, the tires are bald, we work the fields all day. What will she do?" In his despair he underestimated her strength and adoration.

"Pop, she loves us, this is where she wants to be." He listened and kissed me. We were very close. Next morning he wrote her to come.

She smothered us with kisses when we picked her up at the Cairo bus station.

With a couple of bucks she knew how to make everything taste wonderful. In cooking she was fifty years before her time. She worked with Italians who taught her every pasta dish imaginable. With a few of our tomatoes, eggplants, and onion she performed miracles.

She knew all about gardens and was familiar with anything that grew. I still remember a day when hand-in-hand we went into the woods and found a whole patch of wild rhubarb, wild celery, scallions and a field of blackberries… With a couple of Wally's eggs, a little sugar, and some flour she made them into wonderful pies.

Mama was also making a new person out of Papa. I still worked full-time for Wally, but Pop only came up three days a week. Mama had the same energy level as he and they were transforming the place… they were making it into something livable.

Once as we picked wild rhubarb together she told me that she was never going back. She quit the job and would rather die than go home alone.

It was almost September and Wally told us to start picking the potatoes. They were ready… so was Mama. With a spade and a heft of the foot we all plunged the shovels into the loam and brought up a bountiful crop. Papa and I shook the dirt and Mama broke them up on their way into the burlap bags. We had hundreds of bags, and Pop made a deal with a wholesaler in Catskill who bought the whole lot. We were rich in 1935!!

The old man had found a way. We went home that year with a full tank of gas, me driving all the way!!

He went back up there alone in November. He had a wood-burning stove and enough canned stuff and macaroni to get by. It snowed a lot that year and the roads were blocked. What wonderful things he created inside of the house during those days. With the terrible fear of poverty almost abated he could look forward to another successful season of planting. This time he brought up hundreds of Mason jars... that same Department of Agriculture was teaching him new methods to sell his cash crop.

Wally came down in the snow with the team of horses and brought him up to the farm. They were great friends now... they both worked around the barns. He learned to milk cows, and through osmosis was even starting to think like a farmer.

I went up every summer until I finished high school and loved every minute of it. By 1940 the place was transformed into a farm with a sparkling cottage, complete with flowering shrubs, even a small lawn. But the jewel would always be his gigantic string bean garden.

People were working again and a little money was trickling in. Leave it to him, he found pupils in the small hamlet and combined his two great loves... fiddle and farm.

I went into the Army in 1942 and soon after he wrote me that his dear friend Wally had passed away. How beautiful and sensitively he wrote about that old farmer who he had learned to love.

Now in my old age I think of him and marvel at his great courage. He was my ideal, my teacher and my great inspiration. If only I had a chance to thank him for that pot full of green beans.

・・・・・・・・・・・・・・・・・・・・・・・・・・・・・・・・・・・・・・

・・・・・・・・・・・・・・・・・・・・・・・・・・・・・・・・・・・

Close Tolerances

William J. Smart

There are many signs of middle age. One of them is finally buying a house that has somewhere a room set aside as "Dad's Study." By the third house I got one. Actually, it's a small room which the former owner had stolen from the garage. He paneled it and laid the indoor/outdoor carpet a month before the marriage dissolved. Now it's mine. It has taken me sixteen years and two mortgages. It cost $185,000, including the other rooms. So, it is beginning to materialize, the middle-class male's dream.

But one day there was a problem. One day I noticed that people and domestic animals had a way of walking in and out as if it were the kitchen or something. Eventually, some close male friends picked up on it. There was an opening for a door but the study had no door. My close male friends said that the solution was simple. I guess they weren't as close to me as I thought.

In former houses, I had to work in the kitchen. Sometimes, I would pause in the night and watch the door shut. Just to hear it. Waters from the bathroom upstairs, creaks from the costly little sleepers overhead, the sound of the dog's choke chain dragged along the mud room floor next door... Mammals of all kinds take orders from a door, if it closes properly, and if it makes that sound when it closes. It was the sound of brass—the latch bolt as it clicks properly inside a good quality strike plate. My new study lacked that sound.

When I researched the matter, I turned over many disappointments. The library's easiest book, succinctly entitled *Doors and Windows,* one of the *Time/Life Home Repair and Improvement Series,* drove the nail home, so to speak. Hanging a door is a skill not recommended for the home handyman. Traditionally, it is a job reserved for the most skilled carpenter in the contractor's crew because, for one thing, the tolerances were too close for the amateur. Prior to reading this, I had never in my life known disappointment in a library. Cast alone on the beach of my middle-class dream, I considered, for the first time in years, asking my father for help.

· · · · · · · ·

My father was a printer who had quit his formal education at grade eight. Most weeknights, during my childhood, he came home from work around nine and ate alone in the dining room after the rest of us children were in bed or at homework. I used to sneak out of bed just to watch him eat—both of us silent by rule.

He huffed and puffed when he ate. And his hands seemed unnaturally large when they held a piece of Wonder Bread doubled over a couple of sausages. I was appalled by the size of his hands but I was also disgusted by their dirtiness. Clearly, they lived by different rules, these hands. I thought they were uncouth and, by extension, I suppose I thought my father was too.

The last thing a printer does each day before leaving is to wash the presses. Some nights he would be so tired that he would lean on the press rollers and then even his arms came away in bands of printer's ink. His hands summarized the whole day's work in swirls of color. Sometimes he held up his hands at the dinner table to irritate the rest of us, or perhaps just to validate the work he had done all week.

In the summers I worked at his shop, a printer's adolescent devil, grumpy and sanctimonious. My uncomplicated loathing kicked back suddenly one summer evening after I came home from work. Eating alone, I reached across for a piece of Wonder Bread and spotted the printer's ink grime, irreducible in my knuckles and between my fingers. I had been working there only two weeks. So *that* was it. "Honest dirt," my mother called from some other room.

As I was eating, my father came home. He washed quickly and sat down at the table next to me. There was no talk, both of us breathing together, eating our sausages. At one point, I reached for a slice of bread in the middle of the table without looking. I felt something. It was my father's hand—already there. It was inert, waiting—split nails, enlarged and multi-colored—its edges touching mine perfectly. I was amazed to see that, against the whiteness of the Wonder Bread, both hands suddenly looked the same in texture, in size and in color swirl. At that instant, I simply could not tell the difference. We eased both hands back from the bread slowly. For a moment I was too amazed to continue. Then I felt the nudge of his elbow in my side. He smiled slightly, winked, then held up his bread and sausages. Don't worry about it, his eyes said.

Most of my father's day was spent performing manual actions that he had been trained for by the time he was eighteen. Significantly, he had planned to be a piano maker at Heintzman's but he was dissuaded when a tuner took him aside and warned him that radio programs like *Amos N' Andy* and *Our Miss Brooks* would probably make after-dinner parlor music a sound of the past.

On the job, the other pressmen were good enough, but my father had the talent to be boss. No one worked as closely to the swinging arms of the Heidelberg press as it snapped the paper in and out. When there was a foul-up, which was just about daily, the other pressmen would try a few things by rote and then just lean back and wait for him to get wind of it. Eventually, he'd bang through the swinging doors of the pressroom, swear past all of us, then reach around inside the press like a veterinarian. When he left, we were all "useless bastards."

The hands were at their best when they worked at the job he enjoyed most, life at the paper cutter. The cutter was a huge slab of metal, a gibbet painted in baby blue with big rounded corners and red inset buttons for controls. The paper cutter, which we all referred to simply as The Knife, seemed to be a combination of simple and toy-like attachments joined to monstrous efficiency that the adult world seemed to admire so often. The Knife did only what it was ordered to do—even if that meant, as it did on some occasions, dismembered fingers. It was the first object to teach me about logic, brutal and single-minded. When we came in each morning, and when the overhead lights were punched on, they always went on over The Knife first.

Our shop's specialty—if we could be said to have one—was labels. These were small medicine bottle labels mostly, which we imprinted and trimmed and then counted, banded and delivered. Simple, daily and dangerous if you called it boring.

At the cutter each day, my father was as much at the controls, as much in his own personal center as the captain of the schooner during yet another moderate hurricane. He would hum, sometimes even whistle, while the tiny lozenges of stock went in and out of the blade, alternately going up and down, unbelievably close to his fingers, as if he were pushing against forced retirement the only way he knew how. Sometimes, he would eat his lunch at the cutter at the same time as the little labels slid in and out of the blade, coming and going. Sometimes, during all this sleight of hand, he would call one of us over to chat. He would look right into your widening eyes.

Being a printer means working with metal as if it were some other substance, wood perhaps. I never saw a piece of seized metal or machinery that didn't come to after he put his hands on it. There may have been exceptions, but I never saw any, and I was at an age when I was hoping for them daily.

Secretly, I'm sure he revelled in his competence, but today I often wonder why he was never able to teach others how to do what *he* could. Perhaps, at least one of his three sons would then have taken over the family business had he, Prospero-like, let us seize his books briefly. Eventually, his sons would seize many books as they clawed their way through postgraduate courses, working their way through stacks and stacks of print in academia.

At home things were different. Here, he rarely delved into the domestic odd jobs that all dads were supposed to do. In the basement, he kept a smelly burlap bag of loose tools and in the cupboard over the sink we had a dented marmalade can full of rusty screws, buttons, washers, bobby pins, and royal family medallions which, at emergencies, got poured onto a newspaper for panic rummaging and ritual swearing. At home, if the repair couldn't be made with the contents of the marmalade can and a butter-knife (often with some butter still on it), that was "bloody well that."

At home I suppose he managed to render his sons the important lessons on the dignity of the workplace and the need for direct action on the job—*any* job—but it would have been useful to have inherited, as well, the modest pleasure of hefting a good quality tool or the fundamental knowledge of how to square two pieces of expensive wood properly. And I often wondered, even as a child—were these not fundamental skills he should have wrestled from his own father?

· · · · · · · ·

My grandfather was a large, ham-handed man, a circuit Methodist preacher in Weston Ontario at the beginning of a bright new century— Canada's century. Laurier had promised. Without knowing it, my grand-father was missing a university degree. Nevertheless, he was useful to his parishioners because he had his own sleigh and horse in the winter and because, in the summer, he could build small churches and houses pretty quickly. I have a picture of him on my new study bulletin board. It is sum-mer, high noon in the churchyard. He is glaring into the sun, his long body leaning sideways and ready for the camera shutter. Behind him is a large farmer's gate, leaning open and askew. Behind this, the horizon falls off to nothing. Grandpa has the new strap hinges in his hand, squinting, wait-ing to go to work. God's in his heaven.

In the summer, when my father was a boy, he helped Grandpa build the houses. But the winters were worse, he said. Each Sunday, they would go together, father and son, carrying the word of God to three rural churches on grandfather's route. My father's job was to stay with the horses, to keep them warm and fed, ready for the next trek across the fields in the bitter cold. He would sit in the dark drive shed and study the yellow spade of light from the church, wondering how much longer for all this, sweet Jesus. When the service was over and his father came out—always last—my father would throw the enormous fur over his shoulders and off they would go, father and son, silently into the blue air. Blessed Assurance.

· · · · · · · ·

Years and years later, when Grandpa was ill and dying, I used to tag along with my father as he visited his dad each Sunday. While they were both indoors, I would walk slowly around the house that Grandpa had built. I could hear them talking inside, low and calm sometimes, and at other times, more agitated, sometimes shouting. In the garden beneath the heavy clematis, I sat up straight on the outdoor benches Grandpa had constructed out of willow and cedar saplings twisted and bent so forcefully against each other that I was afraid, if I shifted, they would spring apart and fling my ever useless little body into the compost.

As I sat and waited for the voices to die down, I began to look at the details of the house he had built. It amazed me, even as a boy, that a person could build a house with his own hands, live in it and then, at someone else's appointed time, lie down and die in it. Incredibly, I said something like this to my father once as we drove home and his reaction unnerved me. Jesus, the real housebuilder was Grandma, he yelled. "*She* was the brains. Good God! He couldn't even read the goddamn blueprints! He really just followed her finger wherever she pointed!" At this point, the car accelerated and I shut up.

Near the end, about a week before Grandpa's death, something happened that clarified for me, just a little, the link in the three generations. It was one of those remarkable moments during a short life when everything random happens so fast and in such a coordinated way that it all seems planned from the beginning—though, of course, not one piece of it is.

As we were leaving Grandpa and, as it turned out, saying goodbye forever, I found myself alone with him at the bottom of the walk near the garden gate. It was not supposed to happen. I looked up for help from my father but he had dropped back to talk to the housekeeper. Then I heard a sound behind me.

It was the garden gate, a small picket type—hard white paint in the sun, waist-high and level as a tri-square. Grandpa had shifted his weight to it and, as soon as he leaned on it, he began to float slowly over the sidewalk. His tongue went out. Suddenly, he looked like someone's demented relative, popped loose—a slowly swinging embarrassment to our family all over the sidewalk.

But as he swung back slowly into the garden, one foot off the ground, I realized that the gate had taken his weight like a steel beam—not even a creak. When he got off, the gate returned slowly on its own and clicked shut behind us softly.

At that point, he had a little coughing fit—not much, but enough to make my father and the housekeeper look up and come running toward us. I knew I would be blamed for it: for nudging Grandpa, my own dad's father, into screaming eternity at the end of the garden path. As we approached the others, he leaned on me a little heavily and stumbled a bit.

"G'wan! Don't be such a goddamn milksop!" he growled softly.

I tried the word again in my head. What was a milksop?

At that moment, there was no doubt in my mind that he had been warning himself. He hadn't been looking at *me*. Anyway, the others hadn't heard it.

After Grandpa was scolded and ensconced properly indoors, my father walked back down the path with me to the car. As we reached the sidewalk, he turned and threw his standard smile at his father who seemed to have fallen face forward against the window for this last goodbye. Dad opened the gate and we went through together. In the car, he started to turn the key and then stopped.

"Hey, listen!" he said. "Don't let it get to you, eh? It was always one of the bastard's favorite words."

· · · · · · · ·

A week later Grandpa died. In our house, there was dignified regret and relief. He had been "a good man"—a phrase that seemed to be repeated most by friends, relatives, neighbors who visited in the next few days.

There was no big commotion, no flood of tears or unseemly anguish that we had always associated with... well, other types of families. Grandpa had done a lot right in his life and even his hour of death had been "on the British model." Someone even quoted Keats' "easeful death"—"to cease upon the midnight with no pain." There was some tasteful laughter back at the house afterwards, just the right amount. "Just don't fuss" had been one of Grandfather's expressions.

At one point during the polite banter of the funeral gathering, I seemed to be the only one to notice that my father had slipped out. I took my tea and sandwich out to the sunroom. He wasn't there. Then, turning to go back to the parlor, I got a glimpse of a movement through the trees at the end of the garden. He was sitting down there alone. Should I? I looked back into the house. No one was looking, but that suddenly didn't matter. I simply wasn't sure about all this. Mere common sense said no.

As I walked slowly down the pathway between the raspberry bushes, my feet crunched on the gravel. I spotted my father sitting at the end of the pathway on one of Grandpa's twisted willow benches. He looked up and through me, a look that was new and frightening.

"Get BACK! I'm going to cry."

It was as if he held a gun at me.

I thought about it. I had come this far—moved by something new and important in me—and I decided to come forward. I sat on the bench apart from him. In a few moments, he looked up. There were tears forming. "Isn't it amazing?" he said. "Look at this thing." He ran his hand over the curved arm of the bench.

"How could someone build something this beautiful alone? He made a lot of these things. And no blueprints or plans of any kind."

"It *is* amazing," I said.

I waited.

"You know... you both had a lot in common. I know you were different in a lot of big ways but... I can see the connection. I can *see* it."

He looked up at me. For an instant I was afraid that he was going to be enraged by my triteness.

"You've both built something... used your hands, I mean. You've helped me a lot. Just look."

Then I moved my hand over to his on the arm of the bench. Our hands were level and steady. I was hoping that he would remember the incident with the Wonder Bread, but he never said anything about it. In fact, he never said anything at all, even as we walked back together to the others. He may have wanted to explain a lot of things, but suddenly both of us had the sense that now there was plenty of time. Don't fuss, Grandpa was saying.

· · · · · · · ·

It was a heavy door, solid oak, discovered by mere serendipity at the back of the antique store. It took me three weeks to hang the door to the study, working on weekends and some weeknights. Perhaps it was best that all the books made it seem so difficult.

As I worked on it, as the door came nearer and nearer to its purpose, closing out, at my own super discretion, the people and the things I love, I frequently caught myself looking back at the snapshots of my father and my grandfather on the study bulletin board.

More amateurs.

Now the door shuts and it reminds me. Now I see. My father and grandfather's quiet lives were as exuberant and as sensitive and as flawed as my own. They were not mute or commonplace. On the other side of the photographs, much beyond the usual reminiscences of family tales, these were lives distinct from each other and at the same time always folded inside each other, as adjacent as hands. Each day was a swing of forces in and out, talents reflected, forever a borrowed vitality. Close tolerances, the *Time-Life* people called it.

Now, past midnight again, I'll reward myself, OK? I'll lean back from my writing desk, reach up and open the door... wait, then push it closed with my foot. It will swing behind me in perfect silent geometry—and slowly too, like a garden gate I know. I just wish you could hear it.

The Tower Room

C.B. Follett

In the small, hexagonal room,
under the attic eaves,
lives my dead father, dusty
in his stamp albums, whiffling softly
through his silver and black clarinet.
The stalagmites of his life rose
in mystery, dull mystery, I'm afraid.
For I sought shining armor, a white horse.

The stamp albums didn't do it,
cataloged and primly gummed, each
neatly centered within its black lines.
Nor the books. I had better books of my own,
and six blocks away, a full library
of books. The clarinet. That came closer.
It was eerie with unshed music. The reed
still in place, lick, lick, sip the reed.
His lips had been here. His breath
had teased the notes, fingers confident
and agile on those elusive holes.
But I didn't want his clarinet,
or his reed, or his music.

I wanted his bones, his bulk,
and his sweet unjudging.

Buddies

. . . .

Mary M. Alward

I never knew him until he was an old man. It made no difference. I was a young child. So young in fact, people are amazed that I remember him at all.

As a small girl, I had trouble pronouncing my r's. I remember sitting on his knee in the wooden rocker, looking at the rail fence surrounding the barnyard. The colorful banty rooster perched there to ruffle his feathers.

"Say Rooster," Grandpa would say, stretching the r.

"Ooster," I would promptly return.

"No, no," Grandpa would admonish in his quiet, gentle voice.

"Ooster," I would pipe.

Never will I forget the day his patient tutoring paid off.

"Rooster," I spouted proudly.

His response was instant ecstasy. "Good for you," he praised, his voice filled with excitement. He lifted me above his head, bouncing me until I giggled with delight. I've often wondered which of us were prouder of my accomplishment.

Grandpa didn't wear any teeth. They tell me that years before he went and had a set of dentures made. He returned from town, sat down and tried to eat dinner. Unable to maneuver his new teeth, he promptly removed them. The only time he ever wore them after that was when he went to town.

This and his mustache were a constant source of awe. I would feel his bristly mustache with my tiny fingers and Grandpa would pretend to bite me. My fingers would fly in and out of his mustache, trying to avoid Grandpa's gums. This game of tag usually ended by him rubbing his mustache along my soft baby face, tickling me. I would wiggle and giggle.

Grandpa would laugh in his deep chuckling way. Oh, what a time we two did have. Two constant companions. Buddies.

I will never forget the feel of his large work-worn hand, holding my tiny one, as we went for a walk down the lane. We would visit all the animals. Cows, horses, chickens and ducks. Or, if there happened to be a new litter of puppies, we could be found admiring every single one.

After our daily excursions, there was always a reward. This usually consisted of a treat, often picked from a tree in the orchard. Grandpa would lift me up in his strong arms, indicate the fruit I was to pick and let my chubby hand pluck it from the tree. Pride would well up inside as we made our way to the house.

This particular event was always a joy to me. My favorite treat was an apple. Grandpa ate his apples in a strictly unique way. It could probably be called more of a ritual. After the apple was picked, Grandpa would polish it on his grey overalls. Then, he would reach deep into his pocket and withdraw his pocket knife. This article was taboo to me—all knives were. He would slowly peel the apple, being careful not to bite into the flesh or break the bright red spiral of skin. When this ritual had been performed to his satisfaction, he would hold the skin up to the light. Sure enough, it was all in one piece and thin enough my eyes could see through its transparency. "Mustn't waste," Grandpa cautioned.

Finally, he would sit in the oak rocker and pull me onto his lap. This, to me, was the best part of the whole affair. He did not cut or core the apple, but took his knife and scraped some of the juicy flesh onto it.

By this time, my mouth would be watering in eager anticipation. I always got first dibs. I was always first to eat off the forbidden knife. Then, we would proceed to take turns. Some for me, some for him.

This was a lengthy procedure, shared by two people, each loving the other with unlimited boundaries.

Winter came and Grandpa and I would take our walks less frequently. There wasn't as much to see on a farm in winter. Usually an active place, it turned into a winter wonderland of quiet serenity. The animals were safely sequestered in the barns and stables against the winter cold.

Though we didn't see each other on a daily basis, we still got together two or three times a week. My parents lived next door, so it wasn't as if Grandpa was a great distance away. I was too young to make the trek next door alone. I would have been lost in the huge snowdrifts. So I would beg my mother to take me to see Grandpa. She couldn't always do it. Looking back now, I'm surprised she didn't tear her hair out from my insistent badgering. Her patience was unending.

To keep her sanity or because she knew how much we meant to each other, several times a week she would bundle me into snowsuit and boots and next door we would go. Grandpa was always thrilled to see me and the feeling was more than mutual.

Weather permitting, off we'd go. Just the two of us. Our destination would usually be the horse barn. Here we would visit Punch, a bay gelding, and Maude, a black mare. Punch was my pal. Grandpa would hold me in his arms while I patted Punch's nose and he scratched and nuzzled my hand affectionately. Occasionally, he would nuzzle Grandpa, but seemed to be more impressed by the tiny human that Grandpa had brought for a visit.

When the patting stopped, Punch would butt at Grandpa's arm, telling him that this just wasn't acceptable. Grandpa would administer another pat and a few more scratches, then set me up on Punch's broad back.

"Giddy-up, Punch," I would command.

Of course, Punch never moved. Grandpa would be stroking him gently and speaking in a soft, soothing voice. What a thrill for a wee girl, sitting on the broad back of a gentle horse, secure within the arms of a man whom she thought the sun rose and set on.

Other days, we would walk over to the pond near the barnyard. In summer, the horses and cows watered here. The goose, gander and goslings would swim with the ducks, drake and ducklings, diving and splashing. But in winter, to a small child, it was as if the fairies had enchanted it. The ice glistened and glittered in the sparkling sun and I loved to go there. Because of hazardous walking conditions and Grandpa's unsteady legs, we often had to forgo this pleasure.

The most pleasant activity I ever experienced with Grandpa was a sleigh ride. This was the old-fashioned kind, complete with team and sleigh bells.

One night at supper, my parents announced a surprise for my brother and me. We were going for a ride with Grandpa. This left my mind befuddled. I had never known Grandpa to drive. Always ready for an adventure, especially if Grandpa was involved, I eagerly awaited the upcoming event.

I was bundled into my bulky winter clothing. A scarf was tied around my face and heavy mittens covered my hands.

Imagine my delight when the team and sleigh stopped at the end of the lane. I squealed with glee, jumping up and down. It was a double surprise. Not only was I going for a ride with Grandpa, my beloved Punch and his mate Maude were pulling the sleigh.

My father lifted me onto that sleigh. Grandpa was there, waiting to pull me into his lap. He sat on a pile of straw, with a heavy lap-robe which he tucked all around us, assuring me we'd be snug as a bug in a rug. The frost bit at my nose and cheeks as we glided over the snow. Other relatives were on the sleigh. Aunts, uncles, cousins and my other grandparents. I had eyes for Grandpa only.

Several times he asked me if I was cold. I shook my head. I didn't mind the cold. I was on an adventure, straight out of a storybook. Everyone was singing, the sleigh bells ringing, the sound echoing over the countryside. As we passed the neighboring farms, the people would halt their activities to wave to us, and we would wave back, calling out a greeting. Scenes whizzed by. A man chopping wood, a woman taking stiff, frozen sheets off a clothesline, children sleighing down steep hills covered in blankets of snow. What a joy! All of this and my beloved Grandpa holding me tightly, protecting me from the cold.

That's the last memory I have of an outing with Grandpa. One day, my mother explained to me that Grandpa had to go away. He wouldn't be able to come back. My heart filled with sadness, but Grandpa had already talked to me about it. He'd told me not to be sad. He would be in a better place.

Mother continued to explain that Grandpa hadn't gone yet, would I like to see him before he left? Grandpa! Would I?!

My mother and I went next door and she ushered me into Grandpa's bedroom. His weak, tired eyes caught sight of me and a smile touched his lips. He patted the bed beside him and I scrambled up, wrapping my arms around his neck and laying my head on his chest, his big arms holding me tight. He stroked my face and held my smooth hand in his big work-worn one. I ran my fingers over his bristly mustache and giggled at the feel of it. Grandpa smiled.

"Remember our talk?" he asked.

I nodded my head. Those were the only words spoken that day. No others needed to be said. We were buddies. All was understood without being said.

Finally, Grandpa slipped off to sleep, still holding my hand. I cautiously withdrew it, being careful not to wake him. I slid quietly off the bed and tiptoed to my mother who stood waiting in the doorway.

"Grandpa's sleeping," I whispered. "He's real tired."

There was some discussion as to whether or not I should be allowed to go to the funeral home. I feel my mother won that battle for me.

She dressed me in my prettiest dress, long white stockings and patent leather shoes. I don't recall much about the funeral home itself. When I looked down at Grandpa from my mother's arms, he looked as if he were asleep. A deep look of peace and serenity was on his face. As for me, there was no fright, only contentment.

My Grandpa lay in a polished oak coffin that glistened in the light. The lining and pillow were made of shiny, white satin. I reached down and ran my hand along the cool, smooth cloth of Grandpa's pillow. I turned to my mother, a smile on my face.

"Grandpa has a real pretty bed," I whispered. "He'll sleep really good in that pretty bed."

My soul was at peace. Grandpa had a pretty bed. Grandpa had prepared me for his death. His reassurance that he was going to a better place made up for his loss.

Throughout my life, fond memories of Grandpa have lingered in my mind. I will never forget this kind, gentle man who took time to laugh and play with a little girl. We were buddies in life and remained buddies after his death. He taught me that death was a part of life and he taught me the true meaning of love.

My Father at Eighty-Five

Robert Bly

His large ears
Hear everything.
A hermit wakes
And sleeps in a hut
Underneath
His gaunt cheeks.
His eyes blue, alert,
Disappointed
And suspicious
Complain I
Do not bring him
The same sort of
Jokes the nurses
Do. He is a small bird
Waiting to be fed,
Mostly beak—an eagle
Or a vulture, or
The Pharaoh's servant
Just before death.
My arm on the bedrail
Rest there, relaxed,
With new love. All
I know of the Troubadours
I bring to this bed.
I do not want

Or need to be shamed
By him any longer.
The general of shame
Has discharged
Him, and left him
In this small provincial
Egyptian town.
If I do not wish
To shame him, then
Why not love him?
His long hands,
Large, veined,
Capable, can still
Retain hold of what
He wanted. But
Is that what he
Desired? Some
Powerful engine
Of desire turns
Over and over
Inside his body.
He never phrased
What he desired,
And I am
His son.

Grandfather's Watch

Thomas R. Verny

I lift up my grandson Tobin, press him tight against my chest and plant a big kiss on his shining cheeks. He gives me a quick mischievous smile then notices a bird in the garden and points to it. I carry him close to the tree where a bright red cardinal is chirping away. As we approach, Tobin starts flailing his hands excitedly and the bird flies away. I put him down on the grass. This is unfamiliar territory for him. Tobin surveys it closely then looks up at me and reaches for my hand. I take his soft, pudgy little hand and we walk together. He, a bit unsteady and jerky and me stooped, taking tiny steps and feeling like a giant beside his 14-month-old frame. After he tires of walking we sit down on the patio. His eyes fall on my wristwatch. He points to it. I take it off and place it in his hands. Tobin scrutinizes the watch slowly, carefully and methodically. I marvel at his ability to focus so utterly and completely.

He looks wonderfully sweet and innocent. I would like to charge his batteries up with love and self-confidence and optimism, just like my grandfather, long ago, did for me. Though I don't remember much about my grandfather, I am filled with grief and longing every time I think of him. I miss him. I miss the smell of his cigar, the spats on his shoes, his hands on mine, his intelligent eyes looking at me with love and delight. I miss spending the weekends at his place where I had my very own room full of toys. I remember pumping for hours a many-colored spinning top, watching it go round and round, trying to make it turn forever. I remember a miniature white convertible with red leather upholstery and fat, black, rubber tires. The car had a steering wheel that I could turn and even a gear shift. It was the best toy in the whole world. Today, it reminds me of an early Corvette.

I have always wanted to own a car like that. I probably never will.

My grandfather had an extensive collection of clocks. He had Swiss cuckoo clocks, clocks with long pendulums in tall cabinets and all sorts of old clocks that creaked and groaned as they moved. Every hour on the hour the house came to life with the chimes, bells, whistles and bird sounds of the various clocks. He also owned several pocketwatches with gold chains and wristwatches of many shapes and thicknesses. He explained that the desirable watches were the slim ones because they were the most difficult to make.

Several years ago my mother showed me some jewelry she had inherited from her parents. As I looked over the various pendants, brooches and bracelets my eyes fell on an old, tank-type watch with a faded yellow face and over-sized black Arabic numerals. I asked her if I could have it. She pointed out that the watch lacked a manufacturer's name and that it was not pure gold but only gold-plated. It was also broken and the leather strap was long gone. She could not understand why I would want it. Anyway, I insisted and she gave it to me.

I searched the city for a watchmaker who would either repair the mechanism or remove it and replace it with a battery-operated one. After countless disappointments and dead ends I finally succeeded in finding an old European watchmaker who was able to fit the right mechanism into the wafer-thin and slightly curved housing. Then I had a black leather strap put on it. Now, it looks and works like a charm. Of course, I don't wear it too often, only on special occasions.

The watch, my only palpable connection to my grandfather, is my most treasured possession. When I wear it, I feel more grounded, more complete. Sometimes, in a quiet moment, just before going to sleep, I'll light a candle, darken the room, take out grandfather's watch and hold it in my hands. I am with him again. I am holding on to his hand. It is winter and very cold. The streets are blanketed with snow and there's a stillness in the air, a muffling of street noises that always seems to accompany the arrival of new snow. My grandfather is wearing a long black woolen coat with a fur collar. We are going into a soda pop factory. I am mesmerized by the sight of hundreds of glass bottles passing in front of me on a conveyor belt; siphons fill them with colored liquids. When we finish the tour grandfather buys me a cherry drink. It is a moment full of magic, mystery, wonder and delight. No child ever enjoyed a bottle of pop more than I did. At that moment my grandfather was to me the most awesome and powerful man in the whole world. And I was his grandson. There was nothing the two of us could not do. Together, we were invincible.

When I was about four or five years old, on account of my poor appetite and consequent small height my doctor suggested to my parents that I spend a couple of weeks in the "fresh air" of the Tatra mountains. My grandfather offered to take me by train to this children's hostel. After we arrived there, he checked me in, kissed me good-bye and left. I was terrified. I cried for a very long time. Then the staff marched us out into the "fresh air" in double file. I continued to feel totally forlorn and miserable. Not far from the hostel, I caught sight of a man sitting on a bench, his face hidden by a large newspaper. I instantly recognized my grandfather. Of course, he stayed behind, to make sure that I was OK. Suddenly, I felt much better. I was no longer alone, my grandfather was watching over me. Nothing bad could befall me.

Even during the war my grandfather looked out for me. Through his many connections he received a special dispensation that proclaimed his printing press essential to the war effort. Thus he was able to live and work in Bratislava and from time to time managed to send my parents in Budapest a Persian rug or some jewelry. My father would sell these objects at a fraction of their real value and use this money to pay Margitka, the lady who cared for me while I was in hiding in Budapest.

Oh God, I feel this incredible pull on my heart. I am dropping down, down into a dark abyss. I see my grandfather astride a horse, tall and proud, wearing a First World War Austro-Hungarian Empire cavalry officer's uniform complete with sword. Now he unsheathes his sword, gives the command and five hundred men charge the enemy lines. The noise is deafening, the smell of gunpowder permeates the air. When the dust settles, the enemy is routed. At the end of the day the Kaiser himself will pin a medal on my grandfather's chest.

If I could afford it I would love to have a wood-paneled study in my house, lined with books and with a fireplace over which I would mount an array of ancient rapiers, cutlasses and sabers.

Several weeks ago a friend of mine told me about a fantastic psychic he consulted recently. He insisted that I see her. As a lark, I agreed. At the appointed hour I knocked on the door of a small dilapidated house with a large sign proclaiming "Madame Olga—Psychic Readings." A grey-haired woman, somewhat stout and with pronounced Slavic features, beckoned me into a room lit by a single candle atop a round coffee table. As soon as we were seated across from each other she started to tell me about my life. She was astonishingly accurate in most matters. Then her expression changed and she said, "I see an older man near you. He is wearing a woolen coat with a fur collar, a hat and he is smoking a cigar." She made a sweeping motion of her hand, as if trying to clear the air in front of her. She continued, "I have a feeling that he loves you very much and that he always watches over you." Madame Olga opened her eyes and looked at me, really looked at me for the first time. "Do you know this man?" she asked.

After serving in the army, my grandfather returned to Bratislava in 1918 and wanted to study medicine. However, his family was very poor, the closest medical school was in Vienna and they could not afford the tuition. So he became a printer's apprentice. Soon after qualifying he started his own printing press and he became highly successful. According to my mother he was the first person in Bratislava to own a motorcar and his house was one of the first to have electrical lighting.

As a small child I would often spend the weekends at my grandparents' house. After lunch I would lie down and my grandmother would tell me a fairy tale. To this day I love fairy tales. Once a photographer came and took a portrait of my grandfather and me. The photograph hangs on the wall of my study now. I look about three or four years old. I am wearing a blue velvet suit with a white pocket handkerchief and a white frilly shirt. My grandfather is in a dark suit and bow tie. He has a black mustache and a very bald head with a bit of closely cropped gray hair along the temples.

My shoulders are at the same level as his so our heads are side by side. I guess I must have been sitting on a pillow placed on his lap. We both look serious yet there seems to be, to my eyes, a faint smile on his face. His ever-present cigar is not in the picture but I remember its aroma very well. The moment you entered grandfather's house, you could smell it instantly. It was a fine, reassuring smell to me.

All the holidays we would always celebrate at my grandfather's house. My parents and I would dress in our best clothes and then walk over to his place: on high holidays you were not supposed to take a streetcar or any other form of transportation.

At Chanukah we would sit around the large dining room table covered with a white damask tablecloth set with white and gold Rosenthal china (my mother would say, "the best") and heavy silver cutlery with grandmother's initials on it, part of her dowry, as was the tablecloth and most of the linen in the bedroom. My grandfather sat at the head of the table. In the center of the table stood the menorah, a nine-armed candelabrum. Once my grandmother lit the candles and said the blessing, grandfather would take over and direct the reading from the prayer book supplied to each person at the table.

At Passover time my grandfather would pour an extra glass of wine for the prophet Elijah and open the doors so he could come in. The prayers were always concluded by everyone saying: "Next year in Jerusalem." No mention, not even a hint, of other more sinister places like Dachau, Treblinka, Auschwitz or Babi Yar. No, that was in the air but not as yet part of our vocabulary.

Sometimes, when I sit like this, I feel drawn into a whirlpool of dark emotions. If I give in to it, I will drop down, down into a place from which I'll never return. Only with considerable effort, exerting all my will-power, do I manage to bring myself back into my living room, to the flickering candle, to the sound of grandfather's watch ticking in my hand.

That night I have a really jarring dream about a toilet. The toilet is on a little platform, about six inches above the rest of the bathroom. The bathroom opens up into the living room. The toilet cover is up, as usual, but the underside is encrusted with mud, sticks and pebbles. The dirt looks as if it had been there for a long time. I flush the toilet. Suddenly a torrent of rocks, twigs, earth and sewage surges from the head and floods the bathroom and the living room. I consider taking a shovel and tossing the stuff out the window into the backyard. But then I'll just end up with shit in my garden. Not an appealing thought. I am bewildered, I don't know what to do. I wake up, still puzzled.

I am absolutely certain that the dream is connected somehow to my feelings about my grandfather. But how? There is one particular stone that stands out in the dream. It is egg-shaped, smooth, light brown, the size of two fists and very solid looking. It reminds me of a stone given to me several years ago in a meditation workshop. The purpose of the stone was to help us explore our king archetype. We meditated on meeting our king in the woods. I fell asleep. Needless to say, I did not meet my king. I brought the stone home and then threw it out. Is there a connection between the workshop and my dream?

There's something here I have not dealt with. Something in me that has been deadened, ossified, petrified. Old stuff from deep within me is finally being dislodged and entering my living room, my life.

Late in 1944 the SS broke into my grandparents' house, packed them into cattle cars and shipped them to Auschwitz. Because of their advanced age they either died on the way or were killed in the gas chambers soon after arrival. If I allowed myself to feel their suffering, their humiliation, their degradation, I would die this very instant.

Like the wolf in Little Red Riding Hood, I can feel the stones in my belly weighing me down. It occurs to me that what I need to do is take all these stones from my dream, my toilet, my belly, take them out and place them as markers over the tomb of my grandfather. Let the stones honor him there, not here, not in me.

The following Sunday when Tobin comes for a visit, we go out into the garden and together we dig a small grave under an old cherry tree. When that's done, I take out from my night table a hand-carved walnut box made in Czechoslovakia, find a piece of blue velvet cloth and wrap Grandfather's gold watch in it. I tie it with a red ribbon and place it inside the wooden box. I go back into the garden and while Tobin looks on, I gently lower the box into the grave. I cover the box with earth and stones. Then I say the Kaddish (the Hebrew prayer for the dead). Tomorrow, I will plant flowers and shrubs around the grave. Then at last, while his ashes lie dispersed over the barren and hostile Polish landscape, his soul will have found a resting place. Here, I and my family will honor his memory and pray for his safe journey into the presence of God.

There Is Nothing Wrong With Being Afraid

Elisabeth Spaude Aubrey

I was only 13, a young 13, the last time I saw my father. He has been so much a part of my life that that fact was forgotten and pushed out of my consciousness. On a cold January night in 1945 he and I were walking, my hand in his, inside the pocket of his overcoat, among piled-up snow on a small train station platform of a small German town. We were waiting for the train that would take him to the "front." He had been called up. He was 56.

My earliest memories are linked to my father, holding me in his arms, dancing around the kitchen singing "Pueppchen, du bist mein Augenstern" (Little doll, you are the star of my eyes). As he waltzed faster and faster his slippers would come off and slide under the cupboard. When the dance was over I would lie on the floor and retrieve the slippers and put them back on his feet. We lived in a small village, no store, post office or pub, just a one-room school and little church. Our entertainment was home-made. We had no radio. My father was an opponent of Hitler and did not want my brother and I indoctrinated. This isolation worked for I did not hear Hitler speak until 1951 when I lived in Wales and heard a recording.

Books played a large role in our lives. Winter evenings my father and mother (my brother was in the navy by that time) would be sitting by the tile heater. Shutters tightly closed so no light would show and attract enemy planes, my mother knitting or darning socks and my father reading a book to her. My bed was on the couch because coal was rationed and there was not enough to heat the upstairs bedroom. I was very grateful for this short-age for my father was a good reader. Many times my mother's fingers would be still and my heart would be racing during a dramatic passage. I remember late evening walks to the next village where my father helped the village clerk keep village records and such, unbeknown to the villagers of course. Those walks were lessons, wonderful lessons about constellations on a starry night, or continents of the world, their countries and capital cities. I learned about the workings of democracies compared to reigning monarchs or dictators.

He would not tolerate words like "I can't." I remember saying quite glibly, well, I can't jump over this house, can I? His answer would be let's look at this problem. You want to get over the house. You could put a ladder up to the eaves and climb over, or have a rope tied around your waist and be hauled over. There are different ways to approach any problem. To me he seemed completely fearless and therefore I felt safe when I was with him. The thought of going through the forest sent shivers down my spine but when my father was with me I had no hesitation. Walking just in front of him I was "covered." His eyes on the path in front of me and his body the shield that protected my back—there was no better place of safety. There was a swamp in the forest. We passed it on some Sunday walks. It was a mysterious and eerie place. Walking back from the next village on late evenings with my father I could see flickering lights dancing in that area. I believed that fairies with fancy lanterns were going about their night's work. The swamp was surrounded by a dense tangle of vines and bushes. I remember one Sunday when we crawled through this barricade to emerge into a world such as I had never seen. My father motioned to me to be very still. There on mounds slightly above water were waterfowl of every shape and size. Mothers with strings of little offsprings were swimming among the reeds and bullrushes not taking any notice of us. In whispers my father identified the various species for me. Every color of the rainbow seemed to be represented. Plumed headgear or beauty spots on cheeks were something I had never seen on bird or fowl before. The air was filled with sound.

I stood in awe but also in fear. Stories of lost people following the lights at night only to sink and never be seen again came to mind. My friend's grandmother would hold us entranced with ghost and swamp stories. My father seemed to know the swamp well, knew where it was safe to stand, so cautiously I followed as we looked around. I saw my first heron standing on one leg looking haughtily about, completely ignoring us. Suddenly his long beak stabbed the water, pulling a minnow out. He swallowed it in one fluid motion and resumed his haughty stance. What an unbelievable wonderland, like a dream. Water was seeping into our shoes and we crawled back out to my waiting mother. After the first "look at the state you are in," her eyes met my father's and she just smiled and shook her head. This visit only increased the mystery of the swamp for me. Had I not seen strange and wonderful creatures? Now I could picture in my mind the paths and meeting places of the fairies with their lanterns. No scientific explanation could erase this picture.

My father was a slight man by today's standards but had tremendous strength and endurance. At 50 he could still outrun, outjump or outlift anyone. Until a much younger and bigger new blacksmith came, he was the only one who could lift the big anvil in the smithy. I loved to go there with him to see a horse being shoed. A visit to the smithy was a privilege not to be taken lightly, not a place in which children could run around. I would stand quietly to the side watching. The bellows would fan the flowing embers into flames. The horseshoe would be placed into the red coals with long-handled tongs, to be checked at intervals while the blacksmith cleaned and trimmed the horses' hooves. He had such interesting tools and wore a wonderful leather apron. The glowing horseshoe would be placed on the anvil and pounded into the right size for each horse. Then came the anticipated moment when the shoe was put on the hoof, sizzling and filling the air with a pungent odor. The blacksmith held the special nails in his teeth and now took them out one by one hammering them into the hoof to keep the shoe in place. My father would hold the horse-stroking and quieting it. Sometimes I was allowed to lead it back to the stable.

My father was the unofficial veterinarian in the village. Some nights the watchman would come and waken him to look at an ill animal or to assist at a difficult birth. Some evenings I would be allowed to help, my fingers being smaller, to push a syringe under the skin of a horse to get to the root of a sore. I had lots of nightmares as a child, and even now there is the odd night of bad dreams. Waking up in a cold sweat, with pounding heart I would cry, "Papa, take me in your arms" and stumble to his bed. With my head on his arm I would be instantly asleep again. My mother decided that I was old enough to stay in my bed—after all they were close by. The night came when my cry was answered by my mother's "We are right here, go back to sleep." Alas, there was no sleep for me. I don't remember another night like that, so maybe I was allowed back to the safety of father's arm. I never forgot that fear-filled night.

My father was strict but fair. He spanked me once. I was around 4 years old but the picture is still as vivid as the day it happened. My father was riding his bicycle into town 8 kilometers away, my mother was giving him a list of things to get. We grew most of what we needed: meat, vegetables, fruit and wool from our sheep. When my parents were married they still grew flax, my mother spinning and weaving the linen, my father setting up the big loom and stretching and calculating the warp onto it. I only remember seeing the big loom once at a friend's house, the grandmother moving the foot pedals without once looking at her feet, the shuttle flying sideways between her hands at a tremendous speed. Looking up at my father as he swung the backpack over his shoulder I said, "Will you bring me a ball, a big ball, please?" my arms forming a circle. My father lifted me up for a good-bye hug and said, "I'll buy you the biggest ball in the store." The day dragged on as I kept watch for his return. With the passing time the size of the ball grew. I could envision barely being able to lift it, it was so big. Finally my father got off his bike and I followed him through the porch into the kitchen, hardly able to contain my excitement. He unpacked the pack and handed me my ball, saying, "I am really sorry, this was the biggest one in the store." I was stunned. The ball was not much bigger than my father's fist. Disbelief turned to rage. I ran outside, threw the ball in a ditch and returned screaming and kicking the kitchen door. My father opened the door, saying, "Stop that. There were only four balls in the store and this was the biggest. Next time I go to town I will get a bigger one." But there was no appeasing my rage. I continued screaming and kicking. The door opened again. My father squatted down, saying, "I know you are disappointed, but I did bring you the biggest ball in the store." I would not be comforted. Once more the door opened and a very serious voice said, "If you don't stop now you will get a spanking." I knew about spankings, my bottom having come into contact with my mother's hand on occasion. Still I was on a path of destruction and nothing was going to stop me. So on I kicked and screamed. The door opened a fourth time. My father put me across his knee and I felt the whacks, three, of his belt stinging my bottom. It was not a hard spank, but the fact that it happened silenced me. My father stood me back on my feet and very quietly said, "Now go and get your ball." It was a red ball with silver zeppelins on it.

That night I went with my father to the barn to milk the cow. He let me try but no milk came out. But when I put my hand above his a stream of warm milk spurted into the pail. We stopped and looked at the stars on the way to the house, and I learned that at times we have to accept things not to our liking. Years later, cracked and barely a trace of zeppelins showing, I put that ball in my pocket as I left our house for the last time to begin the life of a refugee.

I was ten when it was decided that I would go to high school. We had talked about high school and university and that I would have to go and live in the city; but in my mind that was somewhere in the distant future, not now. I was devastated. Leaving home, living among strangers, how could my parents do this to me? They must not love me anymore. Day after day I cried and would not be consoled. Yes, I wanted to become a doctor, I had always wanted to be a doctor, when I was grown up, not now. Now I wanted to continue to roam the fields, gather the shiny horse chestnuts or acorns from the big oaks, to wait at the edge of the village on balmy evenings for my father. I recognized his walk coming home along a lane or across a field. Then I would run to meet him. There were always so many things I needed to tell him and he never failed to have a fascinating incident from his day to relate. Go away from home—unthinkable. My body could no longer cope with the turmoil of my mind and I became ill. So my leaving was postponed for a term. It was a time to accept a new idea, to become a little more mature. When the inevitable day arrived and my father said goodbye to me at my new "home," I did not cling or shed a tear.

Every Saturday after school at 2 p.m. I would get on the train back to the little town and ride my bicycle the 8 kilometers home. "Home," what a wonderful word. Coming nearer, I would scan the fields for a familiar figure. Sometimes I would see my father and race to meet him. My mother always had a treat waiting for me. It was wartime and food in the city was scarce, especially fried chicken, my favorite. Sunday afternoon I would have to go back. Often my father came with me. We would ride side by side talking. On those days the 8 kilometers to the train were far too short. On winter days I would ask to be taken in the sleigh with the tinkle of bells filling the crisp air. The answer was always the same. "Sunday is the day of rest for the horses, they work very hard all week." Only in an emergency were they harnessed on a Sunday. Taking me to the train was not an emergency. Exercise was good for me. On those days we would put my suitcase on the toboggan and walk and talk. At times I would ride sitting on the case.

The only time I saw fear in my father's eyes was on a windy late summer Saturday afternoon. I had been told to ride along the highway, not through the bush on a path that we often used. The path cut 15 minutes off the ride home, so it being a nice day I took it. In a small hidden clearing I noticed that the grass was trampled down, like someone had slept there. Stopping to investigate I found a dagger. Near the hilt was a second curved blade like the spur on our big rooster. I could hardly wait to show this find to my father. Since he was not in the fields it was my mother. She went very pale and scolded me for taking the shortcut, making me promise to never, never do so again. I was sure that my father would be impressed with my find. When he came home I proudly placed the dagger in his hand with "See what I found." He did not say a word but looked at my mother and there was that fleeting look of fear. I could not believe what I had seen. My father could not be afraid, he had never been afraid; the foundation of my world was shaking. I looked again, my father was smiling, there was no fear in his eyes. I must have been mistaken; but deep in a far recess of my mind I knew I had seen it. My safe world had sustained a crack. I had to relate in detail where I had found the dagger.

Then we ate our supper and talked of the things that had happened during the week. I reported the air raids in the city and confessed that I had been sent to the principal's office for hitting a classmate. She was a city girl and had been taunting me for being a country bumpkin. I was gratified that I had gotten an A on a test and she a D. My brother had taught me to wrestle to defend myself because I was so small. He would say, "Size does not matter, speed and tactics count." Sad to say, this skill was not only used as defense. On occasion mothers came to our house complaining that I had beaten up their boys. My mother would look at the boy and little me and the other mother would see that the boy's story was highly improbable. My father would have a bemused look on his face and change the subject if my mother questioned me too closely on the incident. We discussed how to deal with taunts. Hitting was not acceptable, was not the best way to deal with this situation. My father said, "We must accept the fact that not everyone likes us, not because of anything we have done; but because we are all different. Not everyone we know is our best friend. We need to accept each other as people."

That evening I went with him to check the horses. There was a new foal to admire. The mare was very protective of her baby but let my father stroke it. It nuzzled my face before the mother called it back to her side. My father looked very thoughtful as he watched them and held my hand tightly in his. The next weeks someone always happened to be in town to meet me off the train. On Sundays my father took me back. We always rode along the highway. Months later I heard that two men killed a farmer in the next village and had been hiding in the bush where I found the dagger and where they were eventually caught. The fear I had seen in my father's eyes was a realization that even he could not keep me safe.

Growing up, I was very much afraid of the Holstein bulls that were part of the dairy herd. These bulls did not go out to the meadows with the cows each day but were tied in individual stalls in the stable. Periodically one or another would break loose and rampage through the village until the dairymen would catch the culprit and ride him back to the stable. Not very dangerous, no one had ever been hurt, but I was terrified. Sure that one day I would meet up with a rampaging bull. One lazy summer afternoon with everyone in the fields, it happened. I was crossing the barnyard when I heard the bellowing, and there was the bull. Running for my life, I automatically turned into the shortcut to our house while the bull stampeded down the road. I swear that I felt the hot breath of that beast on the back of my legs. I sobbed out my terror to my mother.

When my father came home that evening my eyes were still red and swollen. I sat on his knee and with his arms around me he retold the terrible ordeal. Every evening before going to bed my father would go to the stables to check on all the horses. Had they been fed, were there any sores to tend, did the men have any problems that day. Often there was laughter and stories of younger days and first teams. I loved to go with my father, loved the smell of horses and the leather harness and the stories. But not that evening, for in the stable was that terrible creature—the bull. When my father took my hand and said, "Let's go to the stable," I refused with, "I don't feel like it, I am really tired." My father said there was nothing wrong with being afraid. But when that fear rules you, you have lost your freedom and you are a slave. The fear of that bull will grow until you will be afraid to go outside. Then the safety of your house will also be your prison. We went to the stable. My father handed me a little hay and opened the door of the enclosure. There was the bull, tied up but calm but I was shaking with fear. I looked from the bull to my father—no, I did not want to be a slave. With pounding heart I squeezed beside the big beast and gave him the hay. When I came out my father looked at me with pride and without a word slid the bolt across the door. My heart swelled with exhilaration— I had done the impossible—in this one incident I had conquered my fear.

Two years ago I rappelled down a cliff. I am afraid of heights. Through my life I have heard my father's words many times. "There is nothing wrong with being afraid, but...." Some victories have been concrete and tangible like the cliff and the bull. More have been of the spirit.

My life did not go the way my father and I had planned. Being refugees we lost everything, no one wanted us and there was no money for university. In a strange village I would stand by a road waiting for him to come home as I had done many times in another little village. Three years I waited and then heard that he had died from wounds. Not instantly killed by a bullet but slowly wasting away only two months after that cold January evening when we had said our goodbyes. He was not invincible after all, but his words and inner strength live on.

Conversion

Charlotte C. Gordon
(Dedicated to my father)

Perhaps he was fourteen,
it was June and outside
birds sang. Red, green, and blue
on the floor, in the air, on the seats
of the pews dazzle
my father's eyes—the smell of the leather,
old smoke—the sound of the birds
and from above and behind the organ
the notes of a solemn pump organ. No human sound

Only the first low chords
heard by the son
of a son of a conductor,
clarinetist at the court of the Tzar.
Some languages he knew:
Russian and Hungarian and Jewish
Ukrainian and Polish and German.

My father lived with his mother
in the old Park Hotel.
And maybe he cried, or maybe
the master came down from the loft
and said, "Come sing."
And my father saw the names fastened on pews

shine as he climbed the stairs
up to the rays of the light
splintering to bright red and blue.
The plaques on the pews shining
the names of the singers and he—he was here—
far from the hotel and his mother. Why not

Be here where even the sun is red and deep blue, distilled
by this people, altered—why not act old—be old—forget
the stench of the Russias—forget the sound
of his mother's *kibbitz* and *borscht, di Kartofl
un Khalah, zi Kholmt.* Sing her away.
Sing it away. Be an angel
up in the loft. An angel lifting
your voice, lifting in praise of your Father.
Sing with your blood, your youth,
the blood of your children away.

         For no Jews we
are straight white arrows with new names
and a mother who goes back to the Pilgrims,
the heartbeat of horsethieves and Mathers.

And you, you nap on Sundays, an old man
who pushed the doors open, rinsed
his fingers in the baptismal font,
hoping—   But it is still there
in me, my sisters, and in you, my father, it is
thickest and purest in you.

You stay home and you sleep.
You sleep while our mother goes out
in the morning. And your daughters, they all of them

marry—They marry the Jew and raise their sons with Shabbat.
They say *Baruch atah adonai* while you sleep
through mother leaving for where
the light alters to red, green, to blue, and you, you thought
you could sing—sing away
what is here still—in me and in you—our hymn,
the hymn of a boy of fourteen or fifteen
washing the blood of a clarinetist
at the court of the Tzar.
He can do nothing, this boy. *Zi Kholmt.*
He sings with the voice of a Jew.

My Father's Gold Tooth

Sandra Collier

My father had a gold filling, right in the front of his mouth. It was on the left hand side when you looked at him, next to his two front teeth. It was like a frame of gold; it outlined the whole side and bottom of his tooth.

I seem to recall that at one time, an earlier time, when I was very little, he had a whole gold tooth there. That's what I recall, but maybe I am just imagining that. But somewhere in my mind there's the thought that he had an entire gold tooth and that he later changed it to a white tooth banded in gold. My mother's influence perhaps? Her attempt to tone him down, make him more discreet?

I've seen gold fillings in other people's mouths. My husband's uncle has several. When he smiles something bright glints out of the darkness of his open mouth.

But my father's gold filling cannot be missed. He doesn't have to smile, *his* gold is visible as soon as he opens his mouth. As soon as his lips part, to speak, to smile, to eat, to yell at me, there it is. The golden tooth.

No one else I ever saw as a child had a gold front tooth. And it is strange that I, who was so sensitive to the differences of my father, so acutely embarrassed by anything that was not like everybody else's parents, or at least my idea of what everybody else's parents were like, was not embarrassed by my father's up-front gold tooth.

In fact I think I rather liked it. I know when I think about it now I like it. I even wish secretly for a gold filling—right up front—of my own, but I couldn't carry it off. I'm too much of the WASPy tweeds and twinset type. Fair eyes and skin, like my mother. A gold tooth would be completely out of place on me. I haven't enough of the gypsy look, not like my friend Rita who has long black hair and wears purple harem pants and bright orange Indian cotton tops and fake silver bangles that chime when she moves. Little bells ringing all the time, saying here I am, here I am. Look at me, notice me.

It was hard not to notice my father. People always did, and I was nearly always embarrassed. I wanted him to be different. To be quiet and color-less, to not make a fuss. I wanted him to be like my friends' fathers, whom I can't remember at all now, so quiet and without personality they were. Not one identifying characteristic has survived, nothing to indicate that here was a person with thoughts or feelings or passions. Perhaps under-neath their quiet exteriors they were thoughtful, interesting people. I'll never know.

My own father was not quiet, that's for sure. He had a loud laugh, he would joke and wink and jingle the coins in his pockets constantly. The coins would jingle and jangle in his pockets, and heads would turn and stare at my father. My father would smile broadly, wink, and do a little tap dance.

I would be nearly dying from mortification. I would try to fade away, to make myself invisible. Oh please, don't look, don't look, just let me be invisible, thanks. Actually, he's not my father. I don't know who he is, we just happened to walk in at the same time. *My* father is that nice quiet man over there, the one in the dark suit. Oh God no, now he's actually intro-ducing me as his daughter, as if that were an honor, oh no, and now he's bragging, he's telling them how smart I am, that I take after my old man, that I stood first in my class, that I'm going to be a lawyer when I grow up. Sometimes when that happened, someone would turn to me and ask what about *you*, what would you like to be when you grow up, and I would take perverse pleasure in answering that I intended to be a movie star when I grew up. My father would scowl at me and change the subject by telling me to recite a poem, or spell a word. Having been as publicly rebellious as I dared, I would toe the line and speak my lines.

My father was very fastidious. Every week he took his clothes to the dry cleaners. Every week he polished his shoes, or had them polished by a shoeshine boy on the street. He would read his newspaper while he stood with one foot up on the boy's shoebox, and the boy would spit on my father's shoes and polish them to a deep shine. There was a color called oxblood then, it was a kind of reddish brown, and my father had casual lace-up brogues that he would polish himself from a gold and brown round tin of oxblood shoe polish. The other day I looked for oxblood in the stores, but I couldn't find it.

Before my father went out in the evening, he would clean his nails with a little silver nail clipper. One part of the clipper had a little pointed nail file on it, and he would carefully scrape under each nail. Sometimes he would trim his nails, the clipper made a kind of sharp clicking sound and little transparent crescents would fly into the air. They disappeared somewhere in midflight. I never saw one land.

My father had beautiful clothes. His suits were elegantly tailored of fine wool. He wore a black homburg in the winter, with a white silk scarf and black overcoat. He also had silk paisley scarves, with colored fringes. He liked polka-dot ties and wore bow ties often, bow ties that he tied himself, not the ready-made clip-on kind. He wore lace-up black shoes, brogues, and dark-colored socks. This was before knee high socks for men, and so my father wore garters, strange black elastic straps that went around his calves, from which there hung a single metal clip. My father would clip his black ankle socks to the garter, so his bare leg would not show when he crossed his legs. He wore boxer shorts, and for gifts I would buy him what he called "loud" shorts. These would be shorts with brightly colored or funny patterns on them.

In the summer my father wore plain-colored cotton pyjamas; maroon was one of his favorite colors. This was before maroon got renamed "burgundy." In the winter he wore silk pyjamas. Usually these were patterned, not plain, often in paisley again, and he wore a silk dressing gown. In the evening my father would change into his pyjamas and dressing gown and he would sit at the far end of our long gray couch and watch television. My mother would sit at the other end of the couch, and I would sit somewhere in the middle also in my pyjamas and dressing gown. Once in a while my father would say, "Come here, Kiddo," and he would give me an Indian rub, which was a hard rubbing across my scalp with his knuckles. It hurt a lot, and I always hated it.

My father was never gentle with me. His way of being close physically was by rough play. I guess he didn't know what to do with a girl. So we would wrestle, or arm wrestle. My father taught me a lot of wrestling holds: arm holds, leg holds, neck holds. "Be careful with this one, you could break someone's neck," he'd say, during a particularly painful hold which consisted of him standing behind me and putting his arms under my armpits and then lacing his hands together on the back of my neck, pushing my head forward and down into my chest. I'd be pushing back with all my might, and eventually, out of frustration, I'd start bucking, trying to toss him over my head. I'd be no match, of course, and at that point he'd flip me down, throw himself over me, pin my shoulders down, hit the floor three times and pronounce himself the winner. Our wrestling matches started out in play, but somewhere along the way they would become deadly earnest. I would really try to win. We also would try to hurt each other. For real, not play. My father taught me how to punch him in his biceps with my knuckles pointed. We would punch each other repeatedly, until I would break down and cry from the pain. I usually had two or three bruises on my arms, and my proudest moments were when I saw that I had made a tiny blue mark on his large biceps. Sometimes my mother would tell him to stop, and he would tell her, "She has to learn how a man feels."

I was proud of my bruises. They were trophies. They meant I was tough. I could take it. Take it like a man. I would look at my bruises in the mirror, watching them change from blue to purple to yellow. What hurt the most was to get hit on top of an old bruise, a bruise that hadn't faded away. I learned that from my father. He'd hit me first and then explain: "Always go for the weak spot, Kiddo," he'd say. "Always go for where it already hurts."

My father had his trophies too. Purple marks on his back and chest that never faded. My father's purple marks were shrapnel, shrapnel from the war. German shrapnel, my father would say, taking off his shirt so I could see. "Here. Touch it. Go ahead, touch it. Feel that? Feel that hard piece there? That's shrapnel. From a bomb. Your old man's got pieces of a bomb stuck inside his body. Killed poor Dougie. Right in front of my eyes. Poor old Dougie."

Dougie Petrie had been my father's best friend. He'd lived across the street from my father on Pierre Avenue. They'd grown up together, gone to school together, and they'd enlisted in the army together. But Dougie hadn't made it through the war.

My father killed three Germans in the war with his bayonet. He said you had to get close to a man to kill him with a bayonet. He said you had to get close enough to see right into his eyes. He said the Germans he killed had red eyes—they were bloodshot. He could see their eyes were blood-shot, that's how close he was. He said one of them was crying. He was just a kid, my father said, just a kid, crying. He said that it had been hard to do, to kill him, but then he'd thought of Dougie, of Dougie who'd died right in front of his eyes, and then it had been easy.

"And I pulled my gun back like this, back as far as I could, to get more power, see, and then I put my foot out in front like this, see, and I went at him with everything I had and I stabbed my bayonet right into him. Right into him, right here," my father said, pointing to his belly. "In his gut. Where it's soft. Always go for the soft spot, Kiddo. Remember that!" And my father would laugh and jab me in the stomach, so I'd double over. It hurt when he jabbed me in the stomach, but not enough to make a bruise.

One time my father came to visit me at camp. It was Girl Guide camp and I hated it. I was miserable and lonely and homesick and nobody seemed to like me and I didn't know why.

He came on a Saturday, when he wasn't supposed to. He was sup-posed to come on Sunday. Sunday was Visitor's Day. But my father didn't care about rules, other people's rules. He only cared about his own. Those we had to obey, my mother and me, but my father never cared about the rules of other people.

He came on Saturday. I was embarrassed. Nobody else's father had done this.

The commandant of the camp had to come and get me to tell me that my father was here. She said she'd told him Visitor's Day was on Sunday, she said she told him breaking rules sets a bad example. I could tell she was angry, I could tell this wasn't a good thing, I could tell he was being a problem, and that therefore I too was a problem, that I was to blame for this, that it was my fault that my father was breaking the rules, that it was my fault that my father was different.

I remember following the commandant through the camp to her office. I remember my father jumping to his feet, clicking his heels together and calling "atennshun!" I knew he was making fun of the commandant, and I knew the commandant knew, and I hated my father for coming and making fun.

My father jangled the coins in his pockets and grinned. His golden tooth flashed. "Kiddo! Come and give your old man a kiss. Miss What's-her-name here wasn't going to let me see you! But I told her nobody says no to Mick Bader." And he jabbed me in the ribs and winked.

He told us that my mother and grandmother were waiting in the car, that they wouldn't come in, they would wait until tomorrow to see me, that my mother always went by the rules. "She's a real lady, Sandra's mother is. English. A real English lady. You should hear her talk. Just like the Queen. Sandra used to sound just like her. It was the funniest thing to hear. Made us all laugh. But now she sounds just like the rest of us. You'd never know she wasn't born here, would you?" And my father laughed and did a little tap dance and then he scowled and his face turned dark and his voice changed and he told the commandant she'd better be taking good care of me, and that made it all even worse. I saw the commandant's face get red. I knew it wasn't right, what he was doing, I knew he was saying something he wasn't supposed to say, I wasn't sure what, but I was scared and ashamed and I suddenly wanted to cry.

But I didn't cry. I was tough, I could take it, and I kissed my father and said goodbye and somehow made it back to my tent.

I thought it was over, I thought it was finished, I thought I could just put it out of my mind and pretend I didn't care. But I didn't know my father wasn't finished. He had been dismissed by the commandant. Nicely. Politely. But still. Nobody told Mick Bader what to do.

So when the big old cowbell rang for lunch, I was unprepared for what happened next. I was unprepared for the little group of girls standing to the side of the grove, staring. The grove was the most beautiful part of the camp. There were trees and flowers in the grove, it was where we said our prayers, where we raised and lowered the flag each day.

I was unprepared for the sight of the commandant, standing with her hands on her hips, shaking her head. "Have you ever…" I heard her say.

I was unprepared for the sight of my father, my mother, and my grandmother spread out on blankets, in the grove, under the snapping and flapping of the Red Ensign and Girl Guide flag.

My grandmother was sitting on a folding lawn chair. She was too old and too fat to sit on the ground. She was wearing the black silk dress and black straw hat with red cherries on it that she wore everywhere. It was her "going out" dress. She had light tan cotton stockings on, not nylon stockings, but cotton, so they hung around her ankles in baggy wrinkles. She had a huge plate of fried chicken on her lap.

My mother was lying on her side. She was flipping the pages of a magazine. She was there, but she wasn't really part of this scene. People made allowances for my mother. She was beautiful so people made allowances for her, and I did too. I made allowances for her for lots of things, and I made allowances for her then in that moment. I knew it wasn't her fault, she couldn't help it, she couldn't stand up to my father, she was weak, she wasn't tough like me.

There were bags and boxes spread out, a wicker picnic basket, a plastic cooler, an enormous thermos bottle, enough food for an army. My father was cutting open a huge watermelon.

I could hear girls laughing, I could hear my name, and I knew I was finished at camp. I knew I was now the camp leper, that no one would be caught dead with me now, not even the other losers.

The next day, Visitor's Day, people began arriving right after lunch. Girls went running towards their families, smiling, arms outstretched.

When my family arrived, I kept my head down. I didn't smile. I didn't talk. I was stone cold. But I couldn't do it. I couldn't get through to my father.

I wanted him to be bothered, upset, angry, anything, I didn't care what. I wanted to get back at him, hurt him in some way, hurt him for hurting me.

My behavior didn't seem to faze him. He took it in stride, laughing and chuckling, making little jokes about the camp, the girls, the staff, jingling the coins in his pocket, winking and nodding his head. A few times he'd say, "What's the matter, Kiddo? Cat got your tongue?" And he'd grab me around the shoulders and give me an Indian rub, rubbing his knuckles across my scalp, hard. When I yelled "Ow!" he laughed and stopped, satisfied.

And that was it. That's how it was between my father and me. My father laughed and winked and jangled his way through that day and all the other days, his golden tooth gleaming and flashing.

That night, in my sleeping bag, I got sick. I lay hot and sweating in the dark tent, wishing someone would come, wishing someone would comfort me, wishing someone would ask me what was wrong. But nobody did.

Maybe I have malaria, I thought. My father had malaria. He'd gotten it during the war in Africa. It came back every year, and once a year, for two or three days, he'd take to his bed, trembling, sweating, his pyjamas drenched. He had been shipped to a hospital near Naples. He said the nurses were pretty. He remembered the white sheets of the hospital, how clean and smooth they were, after the mud and blood and bombs of the front, where Dougie Petrie had gotten blown up right in front of his eyes. I would take fresh white towels into my father's room. That was before colored towels and colored sheets. People only had white then. It was from a different time, a time when my father was still a god, my mother was still a queen, and I adored them completely and utterly, with every cell in my body.

It was before I learned that my father couldn't cross the Detroit border, because he'd be arrested by the police on the other side. It was before I knew what had happened in Port Huron, with Dougie Petrie's brother, the same Dougie Petrie who'd been my father's best friend, the same Dougie Petrie whose body exploded into little bits of hands and feet and bits of white bone and red blood and all the hot steaming soft stuff inside.

As I tossed and turned in the dark tent, I heard my father toss and turn in his bedroom. My father never slept through the night. He awoke every night. Sometimes I'd hear the stairs creak as he went downstairs when everyone else was asleep. I'd hear the strike of a match, once, twice, three times, and then the little flaring puff of noise that meant he'd lighted a cigarette. I'd lie in my bed, worrying about my daddy, my daddy, my daddy downstairs, in his darkness, smoking, alone. I wanted to go downstairs, to sit on his lap and feel his arms around me and ask him what was wrong, but I never did.

Not Here

· ·

C.B. Follett

I first noticed
he was needed, in first grade,
when we had to add parents' names
to the accident form.
Please, Miss Carson, I have no father.

Just write deceased, dear. And she turns
to chalk it on the board.
(No one got divorced then.)
You too, Freddy, she says to my love,
giver of Pepsin Chiclets on my last birthday.

Freddie cries for his dead soldier father
and blurs his page.
Our glances meet in mutual loss,
in shame at being different,
in pride at being different.

Mother and Grandmother try to tell me
I look pretty, but theirs is not
the backboard I need to hit against.
In Junior High, I have no sleeves
to roll in perfect flat folds,
no long curved tails to hang outside my jeans.

In college, Fathers' Weekend,
a Spencer Tracy–Elizabeth Taylor event.
Softball, hikes, a Saturday night dance
to celebrate genetic linkage.
All those fond fathers and daughters.
My non-genetic uncle comes and I love him
for doing so, filling in as best he can
with the necessary proud looks.

That same dear uncle walks me
down the aisle, pressures my arm
with confidence. Stands in an empty place
and tries to overshadow for me
that ghostly absence, gone so long,
it had abdicated all shape or myth,
save longing.

Between a Father and Son

Peter C. Samu

To be perfectly truthful, I'm not exactly a spring person. Just because the sun's out I'm not about to drop everything, get out there and burst forth. Who knows? I might pull a ligament or fall in love with somebody. As I can recall, falling out of love has always made me feel like the victim of a practical joke.

These days, I seldom venture far from my home. I don't like the smell of linen in foreign, humid places. And my constitution seems to need that morning sauna to rid me of the toxic substances I accumulate by living uneventfully.

Yet, I find myself in a rented condo in Rustwood Bay, Bermuda, with as few of the comforts of home as any place can have a thousand miles away. Shivah is over, the machinery of after-death has wound down, the lawyers have the last codicil in hand and all urgent bills have been paid and I needed time out. My father has been dead a month and two weeks now.

Last week the island was struck by a tropical storm. I set out this morning, umbrella in one hand and camera in the other, to take pictures of an uprooted tree I'd spotted from the limo when I arrived last night. I found it, about a mile down the road, a thirty-foot yew, lying in the gutter. Rather than uprooted, its trunk was neatly ripped just above the root line. But there was nothing to photograph. The tree was lying on its side, in the gutter, without a hope in Hell, maintaining a sad kind of majesty. So long as the sap was running, it would be business as usual.

I've lost three close relatives in the forty-six years of my life. I guess that's not all that bad. Unfortunately, my son Jeremy was the first to go, twenty years and four months ago. Rachel, who was three at the time, tried to fill the void by becoming superchild. To this day she reaches for the unattainable, deriving no satisfaction from any of her accomplishments. Practically half of my life has passed since the day Jeremy died, but it still feels like yesterday. When the road is slick and slushy, I think of the ride to the hospital on that sleeting November morning, his small body on the seat beside me, rolled up in a Hudson's Bay blanket. I don't talk about it anymore.

My mother died just weeks later. I boarded a plane and flew down to Caracas, loaded down with volumes of crossword puzzles, a hobby that came to me while waiting at the airport. I returned with several of her paintings, rolled up as hand luggage. They now hang in the living room in my house. She hadn't even told me that she'd taken up painting in the last ten years of her life.

And now my father. My friends' fathers started dying off about ten years ago. I used to go to funerals and assume my grieving friend's posture and expression. Would I be up to it when it came my turn?

When he'd turned sixty-five, Opa, as he liked to be called, developed macular degeneration, a condition that eventually deprived him of 90 percent of his vision. One Sunday after family brunch, when he still lived in his home on Old Orchard, we set out for a walk with Rocky, his tiny wire-haired dachshund. Rocky, who was about eighty in dog years, started pulling at the leash every few steps, feigning a sudden interest in dandelions, but the huffing and puffing gave him away. Opa stopped and looked at him for a long time. Then he turned to me with moist eyes and made me swear that I would never let it happen to him, that if he were too sick to end his own life, I would help him. I said of course I would. He carried Rocky home in his arms (the dog lived three more years) and then showed me a hiding place under the floorboard of his bedroom closet. In it was the largest vial of morphine I'd ever seen, enough to propel fifty adults of average height right past euphoria and into oblivion. I noticed the expiration date was only six months away, but it wasn't my place to bring it to his attention. Years later, when I helped him move to Clarissa Towers, it was still there, sediment collecting on the bottom.

The policeman rang the bell on a Sunday morning. He held his hat in both hands, gazing at a point just below my eyes. I asked him in. He suggested I sit down because he had something to tell me. I said I was fine but why didn't he sit down and could I offer him a cup of coffee and he said all right if it was made. I handed him a mug and we both sat down. I figured they must teach this sort of thing at police school. Also, I was in no hurry because somewhere in the back of my mind, a voice told me that I could not slow down the clock, that something had happened to Rachel. At last he pulled out his little book, looked across the table and said he'd just come from Clarissa Towers.

During the war when I was not quite right, I had to go into hiding. One morning, I found myself alone on a train, on my way to a farm in Gyömrö, to stay with distant cousins of our cleaning lady. I was given a new name and a new identity. Now, for the first time in my life, I was grateful for the lesson I learned in Gyömrö, not to give myself to spontaneous exclamations of any kind, or I would have let out a tremendous yelp of relief that it wasn't Rachel the policeman came to talk to me about.

Opa died at 1:34 a.m., the eighth of March 1992, at the age of eighty-eight. I had to identify him later at the morgue. The canvas bag on the stretcher looked very much like a sack of potatoes. He had fallen twenty-one stories from his balcony, landing on the flat face of a rock, chosen at some point in time by a landscape architect. To be perfectly truthful, it wasn't exactly an accident: he'd jumped.

I asked the Rabbi, as I sat in his office the evening before the funeral, if he wouldn't mind touching briefly on the circumstances of my father's death, because I didn't want people to leave the synagogue whispering. No, he said, he wouldn't be able to do it in a way that would do my father justice. Had he acknowledged that Opa's death was by suicide, as I found out later, his burial couldn't have taken place in the synagogue's cemetery, where Opa had purchased plots for himself and Dora, and one presumably with me in mind. But, if I liked, said the Rabbi, I was free to speak at the service without restrictions of any kind.

I knew I owed him that much. But would I be able to pull it off? Would I be mournful enough, or would the words stick in my throat like so much babble? But if I missed this opportunity, there would never be another and Opa's death, too, would recede into another yesterday.

At the appointed time the Rabbi looked up from the pulpit and I nodded, having waited until then to make up my mind, hoping to the very end for a last-minute reprieve. I pulled the speech from my inside coat pocket and walked up slowly towards the Rabbi, doing everything slowly as befit the occasion. I spoke softly so that people would have to pay attention and paused between sentences.

I spoke about the kidnappers and the murderers, those familiar ghosts that had plagued him for years, joining forces that fateful night to push him over the railing. I spoke about his years of persecution, first at the hands of the Hungarian Communists and then the Nazis, of forced labor camps in the Ukraine and of his year in Auschwitz. Here was a man, I said, who had dedicated his long and distinguished career to improving the life of others. That he should end his own life with such violence to himself was not only a measure of his desperation but also a testimonial to his courage. How unfair if we were to judge his action from the armchair comfort of our own morality.

Then a thought flashed through my mind that wasn't part of my prepared speech. I heard myself saying, "My father had a lifelong struggle with giving and receiving love." There it was, out in the open, floating high above for everyone to see. Where did it come from? What made me say it? A choking sensation was rising in my throat and for a moment I felt I was about to fall. Maybe if I fainted, people would think I was overcome with grief.

The thought of Opa as a little boy flashed into my mind. I saw him climbing the wooden steps on the side of the barn, following his grandfather up the stairs to the room they shared. I could see the sun behind the barn, not five o'clock yet, as they were retiring for the night. It was Opa's responsibility to be his companion, sleep with him in his room and keep him company while he studied the Talmud three hours every night and two hours before sunrise. Boys would be playing outside and there might be visitors in the house but Opa couldn't take part.

Opa had often talked about his tyrannical grandfather, but it was only now, seeing them together, that made it believable. I saw three of us going up the stairs, Opa's grandfather leading the way, then my father, then me. Then I became aware of a small person behind me, Jeremy, climbing on all fours, bringing up the rear. Tears welled up in my eyes and spilled over my face. I had help. "You're not alone," they seemed to be saying.

"My father lived in a different time," I said. "It was a cold and cruel place. His parents were poor and they had ten children to feed. Love, tenderness, hugs and kisses had not been invented yet."

There was a long silence after my speech. Did people want to applaud, or did it just seem so to me, as if my performance had surpassed their expectations? The Rabbi thanked me and all at once it was over. People came forward to tell me how brave and courageous I'd been. My ex-wife, with whom I hadn't spoken in years, ran up to embrace me. Finally, the staff ushered everyone outdoors. What was so brave about it? How much had I really loved my father? Anyone in my place would have done the same. Rachel, meanwhile, had slipped into the limo. Was she the one person who could see through me?

Of Opa's many old friends, only Mr. Zsiga is still living. At the Shivah he wasted no time before filling me in on what a ladies' man Opa was in his day. Apparently, he'd liked the company of entertainers most of all. Before I arrived in Canada, Zsiga said, Opa was living with a beautiful Hungarian cellist whose name didn't matter. They went camping in the summer and he would leave his practice and join her for concerts in various cities in winter. But Opa, to his friends' astonishment, married the widow Dora instead, not a beauty by any standards, who owned a spacious home in Rosedale. Zsiga said he'd wanted to welcome me into a stable, respectable home.

Suddenly, I wanted to know everything about the beautiful Hungarian cellist and whatever had happened to her, but Zsiga was looking around nervously. I was able to extract "Julia" but he wouldn't reveal her last name. Had they continued seeing each other? Yes, the affair had continued, he said, for almost ten years until she finally gave up and returned to Hungary.

Then he lowered his voice to a whisper, "God knows how long Dora knew," and vanished into the crowd.

Opa lived his life according to a set of ancient axioms governing men's behavior in Middle Europe. People must take you as you are or to Hell with them; you don't apologize when you're right and you're never wrong; deeds not words are the measure of a man; showing your feelings makes you vulnerable to your enemies. So, of course, he never confided in me about Julia.

In one of my earliest memories, I'm about four or five, Opa is running alongside, dressed in shirt and tie, sweat pouring down his face, his arm letting go, launching me on my first solo ride. It wasn't my bicycle, but from that moment on I prayed every night for a bicycle of my own. In another scene I see him administering an injection. The patient, a husky, muscular man, is bent over, his pants lying in a heap around his ankles. Opa throws the syringe like a dart, with a graceful snap of the wrist that for some reason fills me with tremendous pride. Years later, as a teenager, I remember throwing my switchblade into a tree, trying to perfect that manly flick of the wrist. Then there was a photograph of the two of us, taken when I was about four. We're in the park, holding hands, his eyes sternly ahead, preoccupied with weighty things and me trying to keep pace, frowning, neither of us at ease with each other. This remained, I suppose, a constant throughout our lives.

Did I or did I not thank him for the bike? I can't remember now. Thirteen-year-olds, even those with good intentions, have lots of distractions—Ramona, for one, seated in front of me in class, whose curves and valleys sent my hormones soaring, preventing me from standing up when the bell rang, even though she had a little mustache not quite visible from my vantage point—not that it mattered.

My bike and I struggled up the wild barrios above El Paraiso where even eight-cylinder cars overheated and stalled. Then we turned around and hurtled down at breakneck speed, the wind whistling in my ears and blinding my vision. As far as I was concerned I owned the only Austrian ten-speed in Venezuela, where derailleurs and caliper brakes were to be seen only in Pathé newsreels of the Tour de France. I even gained enough confidence to ask Ramona out to a movie, but she declined.

I wish now that I had told Opa how much the gift of that bike had meant to me growing up in Venezuela. Every night I carried it up to my room, worked on the chain, the gears, and the bearings, learning its workings inside and out and putting it all back together for my morning ride to school. Sometimes I sat in the saddle, pedalling backwards, listening to the chirping of the rear hub assembly, reconstructing old images of Opa, dreaming how it might have been. I was only five when my parents split up and I wasn't to see him again until I was eighteen. Had I really once crawled into their bed, between the two of them, or was that only a dream?

Rachel graduated two years ago with a philosophy and psychology major, with the highest grades in her class. Nothing else would do. Since then she's been crisscrossing the globe on a mission of self-discovery. She phones collect on Sundays, if convenient, from anywhere in the world. I try to disguise my disappointment when she hasn't called for several weeks. How long do I keep her on the line? If only I could keep it light, communicate a positive outlook on the world. But it's not how I'm built. Everything she says fills me with foreboding. The conversation falters. I even allow my "I love you" to be swallowed up in overseas static, afraid of committing too much. What assurance do I have that my love for her is any more solid than other loves I've known in my life? If she really needed me, might I just turn out to be papier mâché?

As Opa's health declined, so did his inhibitions. He revealed things about his past he'd never told me before. Before he and my mother divorced, when I was about four, my mother had run off with a man to Paris. He didn't say it was an affair, exactly. They went for the "Theatre," and the "Arts." He mixed up past and present and sometimes he wouldn't even know he was talking to me.

Last January, on an icy Saturday night, Dora called at one in the morning, crying hysterically that she wasn't able to retrain Opa, that he insisted on going home in shirt-sleeves and slippers. His enemies had kidnapped him and stashed him away in a replica of his apartment, complete with furniture and personal belongings. I rushed over as fast as I could. The moment he saw me he turned on me, fingering me as the principal perpetrator, leader of the gang.

He was shouting, "Murderer! He's killing me! Help! Call the police!" Dora was near collapse and, at my urging, lay down in her room. There was no sense trying to talk him down. I had to straddle the door. There were four bolts which I was snapping shut as quickly as he was opening them. Finally he grabbed my thumb, almost twisting it off, so that I had to take hold of his arm, afraid that we would end up in a wrestling match and that I could do him serious damage. An hour of this and we were both drenched. Then he slumped into his rocking chair, exhausted.

"Opa," I said after a few minutes of silence. "Where's Rocky?" Rocky, his dog, as we both knew, had been dead at least fifteen years.

"He's not here," he said, looking around. "He's dead. Isn't he dead?"

"Opa, remember the house? Remember the walks with Rocky on Old Orchard?" Opa had loved his dog and still spoke of him almost every day. It had been a period of relative calm in his life. I reminded him of his various bridge partners, all physicians except for Mr. Zsiga who worked at General Electric, and of the Sunday morning rehearsals at the house where he and three musicians got together to form a quartet. He'd had to pay the other musicians to play with him.

"I was terrible," Opa said, almost smiling.

Dora, I remembered, had taken a sudden dislike to the cello. Was it when she'd found out about Julia? She made him give it up altogether. The cello ended up in the Hungarian old folks' home where it still sits, probably unused.

"You weren't so bad," I lied.

The tension eased from his face. "Walkie, walkie," he smiled. It was the code that made Rocky crazy with anticipation. But every time I tried to bring him closer to the year of his move to Clarissa Towers, he panicked and bolted for the door. He never did take to apartment living.

Next morning, after a sleepless night, I told him he was free to go. He still thought I was his captor but participating in his escape also earned me points as co-conspirator. He let me help him with his winter coat and we left the apartment bundled up in warm clothing. At first I trailed a few steps behind, but soon he tolerated me at his side and we rode down in the elevator together. He paused for a minute in front of the building, identifying some of the landmarks, but they merely reinforced in his mind the devilish craftiness of his kidnappers.

We walked about an hour, arm in arm, stopping frequently like two old men, a small midwinter sun rising between East and South. Everything was thinly coated with ice. Seagulls from Lake Ontario circled overhead, riding their invisible thermal, perhaps over nothing more than a subway gate. A row of blackbirds sat perched on silver threads stretched between utility poles. The street was still except for the occasional Sunday worshipper walking by, his scarf held tightly against his mouth. Very gradually, Opa's face started to show the intense struggle between delusion and reality.

He yanked on my arm and turned me toward him, looking intently into my eyes. "Tell me the truth. Are you really my son?" And a few steps later, "Then who's this other Steven, the kidnapper?"

I was suddenly aware of my fatigue, while he only seemed to be gathering energy. As we approached the building he pulled away, heading straight for a three-foot boulder in the shrubs, transported from its Precambrian rock bed in the Muskokas. He spread the top branches of an Euonymous bush and tapped the rock's flat surface with his cane. Then he pointed straight up to the sky. "I live up there," he said. "Right?"

As we approached the elevator he insisted I enter before him, tipping his hat as I passed. He was animated and jovial, his brow unfurrowed, as if the madness had stripped his mind of all worry. He told me how delighted he was to discover that he had a son at this late stage in his life and remarked on how much I resembled him. Then we sat in the living room, he in his rocker and I in the middle of the sofa, keeping myself propped up with an arm on each side. He looked at me for a long time with unaccustomed tenderness, like a father seeing his newborn son, full of hope and potential.

"You don't know how pleased I am to meet you," he said at last, smiling broadly. "Did you know that if I hadn't played poker I would still be married to your mother? What do you think about that?"

"Really?" I said. Of course he'd told me this many times. He was always going on about his gambling, although Dora had switched him to bridge early in their relationship.

I felt I was being treated like a rare, distinguished visitor that brought out in him his most charming self. He hopped across the boundaries of space and time with the agility of a laser wand. "You know, I met him in Auschwitz," he said, as if we'd never left the subject. He was referring to my mother's boyfriend. The man was about ten years Opa's junior. He had met him again, crouched on the floor of a barrack, emaciated, only days away from death. Opa went on. "I asked him if he remembered me. 'Do you remember me?' I said. And he looked away and said, 'Yes, but I don't want to remember. And I don't want you to remember me either.' You see he was still feeling guilty, although he had one foot in the grave. He came to tea, you know? She invited him to the house. To my house. She asked and I said yes. Of course, why not? I didn't know, you see."

Opa stood up and stretched himself to his full height. "He was dressed," he wriggled his neck to demonstrate the man's tight-fitting collar, "in a tux, you know, for cocktails, with striped pants. They went to Paris together. Funny, now I can't remember his name." He laughed a gutsy barroom laugh and sat down. "What do you say to that?" Then a cloud came over his eyes. "I hope you won't be offended. I enjoyed your company so much. Now I can't remember your name. Oh yes, Steven! Strange. I have a son by that name."

This is day six in Bermuda. My tree, as I've come to regard it, has not been moved. For the most part it looks perfectly healthy. How do you take the pulse of a tree? When does a tree actually die—when the mortal wound is dealt, or is the signal the last brown leaf dropping to the ground?

I've been eating sandwiches because I hate waiting to be served in restaurants. I haven't been sleeping very well. I find my arm stretched across the bed as if I expected someone to be there. Drifting in and out of sleep,

I think about Opa's cellist friend, Julia. What a beautiful name! She must have known a part of him I never got to know, perhaps the very best part. I should have twisted Zsiga's arm for the rest of her name. It's not too late. I could look her up in Hungary. But in my mind she's a young woman. I smell the resin of her bow when she walks into the room. Then it hits me. If she were still alive, she would be well into her seventies.

Couples still bother me, after all these years. Not so much the young couples, touching and fondling everywhere I turn on this island. Theirs is a one-act play and I've seen the ending. It's the older, gentler folks, the survivors, the ones who touch with their eyes and speak in silence. I recognize them instantly, on a house call or seeing them sitting in my waiting room. There are fewer of them around these days, I've noticed. I used to tell myself that somewhere there would be an ideal woman for me. But chance never brought us together and now I don't even date anymore. Auditioning for the part takes too much out of me.

Tomorrow I'll go to the movies. I enjoy films with large, happy families. Scenes that make the audience chuckle bring out in me a peculiar need to shed tears. Scenes between a father and son or a father and daughter, being gentle with each other, break me up without fail. The more effortless and casual it is, the more exquisite the ache. It starts in my chest and moves to the neck trying to burst up and out of my throat, but if I hold it there, by morning it's gone.

I can't stop thinking about the last moments of Opa's life. The police noted scuff marks on the outside of the sheet-metal railing. He didn't just jump. He must have sat there, the handrail cutting into his flesh, while he was making up his mind. What if he had only wanted to hide from his tormentors, thinking that there was a ledge on the other side and, finding there was none, lost his balance.

All afternoon and evening, according to Dora, Opa had been trying to nail shut the aluminum sliding door to the balcony. He'd told her the murderers were coming in from there. Later that evening, he locked her in the bedroom to keep her safe from harm. Had he already decided then? Did he choose the early morning hours to avoid injuring anybody? But why put on a clean shirt and dress up in a suit and tie? And strangest of all, he'd turned off all the lights, something he would never ordinarily do because he despised the dark.

There was a fresh cigarette stub in the ashtray, a Carlton, extinguished in his usual manner, folded in the middle. I see him smoking his last cigarette, sitting on the balcony in the dark. What would be going through his mind those final moments before the fall? What part of the original circuitry was left? So much of the real Opa was gone. Was it the sane part of his brain, taking charge at that exact moment? What about that frosty winter morning, two months before, when he and I had stood under the balcony. Had he known already then?

We were alike in so many ways. I wondered whether I would end up like him. Would I have the guts when it came down to the wire, or would I let the days, weeks and months go by, hoping against hope that things would right themselves, until the decision was no longer in my hands. If only he had decided earlier, when he had more control, he could have chosen a more gentle exit. How do you know when the time is right?

One morning he seemed in better humor than I'd seen him for several weeks. I decided to ask the question that had been on my mind forever. "How does it feel to be old?" I had to repeat it again, louder. "Is it terrible to be . . . this old? You are eighty-eight. How does it feel?" Was his life really as awful as it looked from my perspective?

"Eighty-eight? You mean a hundred!" He laughed. "No," he said to my astonishment, "it's not what you think. If only I had my eyes, everything would be fine."

At eighty-eight he still saw patients. They would come to him, young and old, go away apparently satisfied and return for the next appointment. I couldn't understand it. It bothered my conscience and I was also aware that any one of his patients could report him to the college. Dora was terrified at the prospect of having him in the apartment all day. She accused me of caring more for the patients, the perfect strangers, than I cared for my own father. What harm could it do? After all, he wasn't doing surgery anymore. As for Opa, he insisted he had to work because he needed the money: he had obligations to his poor relatives, I had no idea how many depended on him. No, he couldn't sell the office building in a down market. "You should have told me to sell when the price was right."

My stay in Bermuda is coming to an end. Toronto, I hear, is overcast, with sixty percent chance of rain, boding well for a seamless transition. While I've been away, my dictatypist has had a baby girl. Hasn't anybody told her about the ozone layer? Life, as they say, goes on. When I get home I must remember to delete Opa's number from my kitchen phone's memory, if I can lay my hands on the instructions.

To be perfectly truthful, there were times on this island when I had fun. For six days I rode mopeds up and down the wet countryside with only a circle of compressed air separating me from certain death. I drank unfiltered water and walked on the edges of cliffs. With Opa gone I alone am responsible for what happens to me. I'm in the front lines now.

I visit the tree one last time. I can't believe my eyes. There are new shoots breaking out at the top of the trunk. But, nearer to the bottom, as I look closely, I see drooping branches, some tell-tale yellow tips, almost brown. No miracles for you this time, my friend. What a gift to be innocent of the knowledge of death, to live timelessly in this world.

The Spiny Beast

Robert Bly

My father and I
Swim a half-mile
Or so apart
In a cold sea.
We know of
The other's pace,
But swim far from
The care of women.
I go on, asking
My shoulders why
My lower half
Feels so heavy.
Only my arms
Lift, the ocean
Pulls the rest
Of me down.
I know that far
Below us
There are old
Model A engines,
Spoked wheels
From horse rakes,
Engine blocks
Broken apart,
Cutting bars, snapped

Ploughshares,
Drive shafts
Sticking from sand,
Thresher pulleys
Scattered on
The ocean floor.
Our failures
Have grown solid
There, rusting
In saline water.
We worked all day
Through dinner till
Midnight and couldn't
Keep the swather
Going, nothing helps,
Drove a piston
Right through the block,
It won't do.
And behind us
A large beast
Follows—four or
Five miles back,
Spines on his nose,
Fins like the
Komodo dragon,
Spiny whiskers,
Following us.

Daddy's Chair

Mary M. Alward

I walk into my mother's house. The first thing I see is Dad's chair. An old wooden chair with four rungs in the back, the white paint cracked and chipped. The seat is polished smooth from years of wear. Not pretty by any means, but Dad's chair.

As I stand by the counter sipping a cup of tea, my mind slips back to my childhood. If he got home before we were in bed, I'd scramble onto his knee for a rare moment of closeness. At these times, he usually told us a story or two about his life.

My Dad was the middle child in a family of eight. A rebellious boy, he left home at the age of fourteen with a friend. Together they traveled across Canada and the United States, seeking their fortune and of course adventure.

Oh, the stories he told at those times. Cowboy stories, experiences I could only dream of. Riding line on a ranch in Alberta, through blizzards and storms in subzero temperatures, the snow as high as the horse's chest, to be certain all fences were in good repair. Living in a line-shack, with only a bunk to sleep on and a stone fireplace for heat. Not seeing a single soul for months on end, his only companion his loyal horse. He depended on that horse for transportation and shared his cabin with him. Eating only what was provided by nature for meat, with a supplement of dried beans, sour dough and beef jerky.

One of his best stories was about his favorite horse, Satan. A pure black stallion, he had once run free with a herd of wild horses on the open prairie. Not wanting to release his hold on that wild freedom, Satan never liked to be controlled by human hands. He'd stand quietly as Dad put the blanket and saddle on his back. When it was time to take the bit in his mouth, he'd shy away, stamping his feet in protest. The real ritual began when my dad's foot hit the stirrup. Satan would rear, neighing his protest shrilly. As Dad hit the saddle, the fight was on. Satan would begin bucking for all he was worth, coming down stiff-legged, trying to unseat him. Every morning as long as my dad owned him, this was the procedure. Satan was stubborn and my dad very determined. Neither one would let the other beat him.

Death Valley, Mexico, Texas. Every one of these places held an adventure. I dreamed of visiting the places Dad took us on these magical trips. His vibrant recollections painted pictures in my mind that made me long to be there. They are still there today and probably will be forever.

Those were the days when Gene Autry, Roy Rogers and The Lone Ranger, Tonto at his side, rode the trails, good guys, administering justice to all who stepped outside the law. They were America's heroes. My dad was mine. In my child's mind I could visualize him, sitting high on Satan's back, traveling the country and turning in the bad guys.

Time passed and things changed. Even after we grew up and no longer lived at home, we'd gather there on a Sunday afternoon and try to get Dad to reminisce. At any age his stories were marvelous. None of us had been far from home and we loved to go on these adventures.

Whenever I went to my parents to visit, the first thing I'd see when I entered the house was Dad sitting in his chair holding the ever-present cup of tea. He always gave the same greeting. "Hi'ya, Doll. Wat'cha been up to?" Then he would grab my daughter Michelle, pulling her onto his knee. "How about a smooch, Pumpkin?" he'd ask and without waiting for a reply, he'd plant big squeaky kisses all over her chubby cheeks. This would send her into a fit of giggles and a big smile would appear on his usually happy but unsmiling face.

When my husband died at a young age, Michelle and I lived at my parents' for two years. Even after we had a place of our own, Dad usually babysat her while I worked. He had been disabled in an accident a few years earlier and having worked all his life, found it hard to be confined to the house and yard. He could no longer do any heavy labor and I feel that looking after her gave him a feeling of self-worth. He needed to be needed.

Later, I sat at the table in my parents' kitchen. Mom was in the garden. Dad and I were enjoying a cup of tea. I took a cigarette from the pack and flicked my lighter, bringing the flame to the end of it. My father sat, watching my every move. As I put the lighter down, he reached over and covered my hand with his work-worn one.

"Why don't you quit smoking, Hon?" he asked.

"I've tried, Dad, I can't," I answered.

"Sure you can," he said. "I smoked for forty years. One day I decided enough was enough. I haven't smoked since."

"Don't you miss it?" I inquired.

"Not really. Only once in a while. In fact I feel a lot better since I quit."

It was an unusually tender moment. For many years, we hadn't been close, sometimes not talking for days. I had been an unruly, stubborn child, and many times that same work-worn hand that had so gently covered mine a moment ago, had connected with my bottom. I had resented it, holding the grudge until it festered. It hadn't been until after Michelle was born, that I realized those whacks were given out of love.

I looked over at my dad and a premonition that he would not be around forever seized me. "I'll do it," I said, wanting to make him happy.

"I know I never told you often enough," he continued, "but I do love you." I looked directly into his bright blue eyes and could see the tears welling behind them.

"I know you do, Dad," I replied, my voice breaking. "I love you too." That was it. The moment of closeness was over. My mother came in from the garden, carrying baskets of yellow beans.

"Blasted cold," my father sniffed, drawing his hanky out of his pocket to blow his nose. He turned to me and gave me a wink.

"Run along now. Help your mother get those beans picked."

I did quit smoking. If my Dad could do it, so could I. Especially if it made him happy. At that time in my life, I'd have done anything in my power to make up for the lost years.

On that fateful night, the shrill ring of the phone caught me off guard.

I grabbed for it, not wanting it to wake the girls. It was eleven-forty-five.

"Hello?" I asked questioningly.

My mother's voice came through the line. "Hi," she said, her voice quivering. "I'm afraid I have some bad news."

Dread washed over me. "Did something happen to Grandpa?" I inquired. After all, he was seventy-five. We'd been expecting it for years.

"It's your dad," Mom's voice broke.

I was in complete denial. "You mean your dad," I said.

"No," she stated firmly. "Your dad."

"No, not Dad!" I exclaimed hysterically. "We were just there. I talked to you only an hour ago. You said he was fine."

"He was," she said. "He had just gone to bed. I was in the bathroom. He made a strangling, choking sound and before I could get to the bedroom, he was gone."

Still not wanting to admit the inevitable, I tried a different approach.

"He just went to the doctor's yesterday. He told me the doctor said he was fine."

Trying to bring me out of the shock, my mother spoke softly. "I know that, but he's gone. The coroner has to come and pronounce him dead. Your brother is on his way. There's nothing we can do until tomorrow. Try to get some sleep."

As I hung up, tears flooded my face. My dad dead? No, it can't be! Not my father. There's been a mistake. This is some kind of cruel joke. But it wasn't and I knew it.

I threw myself across the bed and sobbed the whole night through. Somewhere near dawn, after smoking a whole pack of cigarettes, exhaustion overtook me and I slept.

The next morning, I sat the girls down and told them their grandpa had died. My niece was terribly upset, crying and sobbing. As I consoled her, I watched Michelle. Her face was hard as a rock. She never spoke a word or shed a tear.

Soon after, my mother and sister arrived. We made plans to meet at the funeral home later. My brother was to be there and together we would make all the arrangements for Dad's funeral.

After they left, Michelle went to her room. She hadn't said a word since I'd broken the news. I was deeply concerned. Her Papa had meant the world to her. I would have felt much better if she had cried and screamed. That didn't happen. There was nothing. Just that face, looking as if it was carved out of stone.

Our family cared deeply for each other, though it was seldom demonstrated. Usually, we bickered and argued about something whenever we met. Later that day, as we walked into the room where the caskets were displayed, I spotted a beauty.

"That's it!" I said immediately, pointing to a lovely oak one with brass handles that sparkled in the light. The dark wood, polished to a high sheen, set off the cream satin lining. My father had loved working with wood. It was his hobby and he'd favored oak. This was the casket he would want. I could feel it in my bones.

"Let's just look around," my brother stated. I knew from the tone of his voice that now was no time to quibble. I went along quietly, saying no more.

After we'd looked at several, we all agreed that the one I'd picked originally most suited Dad. We finished our business and left the funeral home, each dreading the task that lay before us.

That evening, Michelle and I chose the clothes we were going to wear the next day. Still, she showed no emotion. I didn't push. I realized she had to come to grips with the grief in her own way.

That night, I lay in bed unable to sleep. Overcome by grief once more, I became angry. Angry at God for taking my father just when we were closer than ever before, angry at my dad for leaving me. From the very depths of my soul, I cried out to my father. "Dad, how could you leave me now? We were so close. How could you desert me?" But deep in my heart, I knew it wasn't his choice or his fault.

The next time I saw my father was when Michelle and I entered the funeral home. At twelve, this was the second time she'd lost a close loved one. Her dad had died of a massive coronary. That time, she hadn't shed a tear until it was over. At the time, I'd felt it was because she was so young. Now I wasn't so sure.

We held hands tightly as we walked up the aisle of the funeral home's chapel. We could see the lovely oak casket at the front surrounded by hundreds of flowers. As we approached, I felt Michelle's hand tighten around mine.

"It's okay," I soothed. "I'll be right beside you."

Together, we stood before the casket and said our final farewells in our hearts, each with her own feelings, not knowing the thoughts of the other, only knowing that our hearts were breaking, both souls feeling an endless void.

The funeral was beautiful. Everyone stayed fairly calm, knowing if one broke down, the others would follow. For once each person was thinking of the others instead of personal comfort, each giving something never given before.

I bowed my head, thinking of standing in my parents' kitchen, as I am now. Once again, I gaze longingly at that old wooden chair. Empty now, like the hearts of those who loved him.

The stillness is broken by Michelle running in from the garden where she's been helping my mother pull ears of corn. At the top of the stairs that lead into the kitchen, she stops. One look at Dad's empty chair sends her flying into my arms, sobbing her heart out. "I miss him, Mom," she chokes, looking up at me, the grief so evident on her young face. "He was the only father I had."

"I know, Hon," I consoled, feeling helpless. "It's okay, I know it hurts. It's like someone's ripping your heart out, right?" She nods her head, her throat too full of sobs to speak.

"It's okay to cry," I assure her. "That's how we let our grief out. If it stays inside, it just gets worse."

"Really?" she asks, looking up at me, tears smudged along her rosy cheeks.

"Really," I reply.

As I hold my sobbing daughter's head against my breast, I look over at Dad's old wooden chair. In my mind, I can see him sitting there, his work-worn hands holding the ever-present cup of tea. He seems to turn toward me, a hint of a grin on his face, and gives me a wink.

"I love you," his quiet drawl seems to fill my head.

From the depths of my soul, I send a message back to him. "I love you too."

Once again, I gaze longingly at that old wooden chair with its chipped paint. It may not be a pretty chair. To most, it would seem to be just an ugly old chair. To me it represents a throne. My father ruled his kingdom from it. I was his Princess.

My Three Fathers

. . . .

Valentina Bek

When I was five years old, my mother and I got married to a man who was a thousand miles away. "Long Distance Wedding" they called it. The ceremony took place in the city hall of Stuttgart, and the only thing that I remember clearly about that day in the summer of 1942 is the groom's chair next to my mother: it was occupied by a military helmet. Had some evil witch enchanted the poor groom and turned him into a helmet? I half expected a golden-haired fairy with transparent wings to fly in through the window, wave her wand over the drab object and change it back into a handsome groom.

My mother had met this soldier in the wine room where she worked as a waitress, and he fell quickly and madly in love with her. I do not think they ever even dated because soon after their first encounter, he was drafted to go to Russia. From there he proposed marriage to her, and she said yes. He had never even laid eyes on me, her illegitimate child, but he had seen my photograph and made the promise to adopt me after the war. I finally had a father, or so I thought.

I have his picture: a strong, attractive face with clear eyes, an aquiline nose, and lips which could pronounce a firm "no" but could also be swayed by a kiss. The two lines running from the wings of his nose down to the corners of his mouth tell me that he was no stranger to pain. Unfortunately I cannot see his hair because it is covered by a helmet, the same helmet which sat on the chair at the wedding. He was a cooper by trade, but in the photograph he is wearing the uniform of the Third Reich, an eagle with a swastika in its talons hovering over his right breast pocket.

The other photograph which I have of him does not show his face at all, it only shows the place where he is buried. There is a beautiful little Russian church, built entirely of wood, and in front of it twenty-three wooden crosses are standing guard over the bodies of the German soldiers who died so far from home. Two small cannons which are meant to indicate that this is the military part of the cemetery point toward heaven.

Then there is the heart-rending letter from his mother. "Dear Maria..." Some of the paper has been eaten away by time. It is the writing of an old woman whose guts have just been turned inside out but who still believes that there is some sense in the suffering. She was told two terrible truths in one and the same letter, my mother's. The first was that her son had married a woman she knew nothing about—he had not even mentioned her name. And the second was that he had died of typhus fever in Russia. Despite her deep sorrow she invited my mother to keep in touch with her and spoke of a possible future meeting.

I do not even have a letter, only a few lines of his handwriting on envelopes addressed to my mother. Since I am a graphologist, these traces of his hand do speak to me, and they tell me that he was a good man, caring and honest, somewhat idealistic and a little naive. The sensuousness which his mouth betrays in the photograph is also expressed in his handwriting. He had a warmth which connected him to the physical side of life and probably made him a tender lover and a gentle father. His attachment to his mother was strong, and it was important to him to live by generally accepted rules. Yet he married a woman who had given birth to a child out of wedlock. There is a beautiful inner logic to his act.

Although he was never meant to live with us, his marriage to my mother gave her the title of "Mrs.," an aura of respectability which in the Germany of 1942 was much more coveted than it is today. I still carried her maiden name, but he was going to give me his name when he returned. I wish... It would have saved me much embarrassment. Another great blessing he left us: a war-widow's pension for my mother and a war-orphan's consideration for myself. One of the smaller blessings was a parcel of heavenly chocolates which he sent us from Russia—I can still taste their sweetness and the sweet feeling that soon I would have a father who would give me presents, hold me in his arms and love me. I would then be just like all the other children I knew.

While writing this story I had a dream in which I was being driven by a man in an army truck. I asked him: "Are you Otto Jehle?" The man turned around very slowly and I leaned forward to better see his face. It was a young face. The mouth was just like the mouth in the picture, yes, it was he, but when he turned more towards me, I was shocked to see that his nose was quite flat, making his face look like the face of a dead man. In my dream I put my head down and howled and howled, feeling both horror and great happiness mixed together in the strangest way.

In the years to come our household, consisting of my mother, my grandmother and myself, was still without a man. They both loved me very much, and I loved them. I adored my mother and concentrated all the love which a child normally gives to both mother and father on her alone. Terrified at the thought of losing her, I resented the odd boyfriend who came to call on her and considered him as an intruder who was trying to steal my mother away from me. She told me later that she had several more proposals of marriage but turned them all down because she felt that none of these men would have made a good father for me.

One of her suitors was Mr. Tag. He invited us to his beautiful house one day where he presented me with a doll in a long box which had paper lace all around the edges. She was a little girl's dream come true, with her delicate china face and blonde hair which could be combed and pinned. But on his buffet he had a stuffed snake in a glass case. That bothered me. I think it bothered my mother, too, and besides, he was too tall for us. We didn't marry him either.

Like most children of my generation, I had not been told the truth about procreation but had been fed a pack of lies involving the stork and little bundles from heaven. He would fly along, they told me, carrying a little baby tied to his long beak, and then drop it into some hopeful mother's lap. Some young women were afraid of the stork, but my mother obviously had received his gift graciously. So why could we not have another baby?

If I couldn't have a father, at least I could have an older brother. The logistics of having that wish fulfilled were not at all clear to me then.

When I confessed my desire to my mother, she proposed that we put sugar cubes on the windowsill to attract the stork who had a sweet beak, it was said. Sugar cube after sugar cube disappeared, and no strong and handsome older brother, not even a tiny little baby brother appeared on the scene. I think it was because we lived on the ground floor, and the neighbor's children ate all the sugar cubes!

Not that I was totally ignorant about men. My mother had three brothers, one of whom I adored, but they lived far away and we seldom saw them. Another man with whom I had some contact was my aunt's husband, a big and very masculine man who used to let me sit on his lap. Leather comes to mind when I think about him. Perhaps it was his uniform.

I never saw a naked male until I was 12 years old and babysitting a little boy. He was only 6 months old, so that the part that interested me most was really very tiny. I was intrigued but not impressed. Even to this day I cannot understand why any woman would want to have such a cumbersome appendage on her own body, contrary to Dr. Freud. I strongly suspect that his theory of penis envy was nothing more than a reaction to his deep-seated vagina envy.

During my school years I deeply felt the lack of a father—it made me different from other children, an outsider in my own mind. In high school I fell in love with a teacher who was forty years old, an elegant and brilliant man who was smoking himself to death. Unfortunately (or fortunately?) he never realized that I had potential as a woman, so my love for him remained a dream. When I found out many years later that he had an affair with a student a year younger than myself, I was devastated. I knew the girl, she was very beautiful with white skin and black hair, bigger than I, more developed, and she came from a respected family.

One time we had to write a curriculum vitae in school, and the day on which we were supposed to read our writing in class, I felt so sick to my stomach that I considered staying home. I went anyway, not wanting to upset my mother, but I hoped and prayed all the time that I would not be called upon to read. All curricula began with: I was born on… in… as the daughter of… and… What could I say? I only knew one half of my parentage, and I certainly did not want the whole class to know that I was a bastard. I had friends there.

As it turned out, I did not have to read. Three decades later, a former classmate told me that all my friends knew that I was an illegitimate child, and the teacher knew it, too, and saved me the embarrassment. Actually, I cannot remember one single instance when I was publicly exposed or shamed, but nevertheless the shame was always there gnawing at my insides.

I used to play with my friends in their garden next door. One day we were taking turns at dancing on a wooden crate, wearing rose petals on our fingernails and boughs of flowering almond in our hair. When the mother of my friend Helga looked out the window and saw me performing on the box, she said: "You have the Viennese charm of your father." This remark set off fireworks in my soul. "Your father." How wonderful to hear those words spoken by a neighbor, almost as thrilling as being called by my husband's family name for the first time. Somebody actually knew that I had a father. My father, my real father, that is, was not exactly Viennese, he was an Austrian born in Linz on the Danube. But I digress. This is the time to talk about my second father, my real stepfather.

After we had been dancing for a while, my friends and I taking turns on the crate, we realized that we could do even better if we had some music. Marina suggested that we ask Mr. Hardy to play his harmonica for us. He lived in the same apartment building where the girls lived, and they coaxed him into coming out. He was a dark-haired man of a slight build, impeccably dressed, and there was a fiery spirit in his eyes. It gave him pleasure to provide the music for our spontaneous dance performance. Afterwards we all talked together for a while, and I found out that he also had a talent for repairing small appliances. So I asked him to come over to our apartment the next day and fix our radio which had not worked properly for years. In order to change the station one had to reach in the back and move a large wheel with the help of a wooden cooking spoon. (This handicap had actually saved us our little radio when, at the end of the war, the conquering French troops marched into the village where we lived then, and confiscated every radio in sight. They could not make ours work!)

So Herr Hardy fixed our radio. But even after it was fixed, and stations could be called up at the mere touch of a button, he still kept visiting my mother. Eventually he rented a room in our building, and then he moved in with my mother while I moved into his room. I felt a little left out, but after all, I was the one who brought him home, I played the role of Cupid. Unconsciously I wanted a father, and besides, I needed someone to divert my mother's attention from me because I was her only love, the apple of her eye and the focus of all her worries.

He first came to us when I was 12 and he lived with us for three years without the sanction of marriage so that my mother would not lose her widow's pension. (We needed the money.) This type of marriage was called an "uncle marriage" and was not uncommon after the war. I called him "Uncle Joseph" and used to sit on his lap while he played the harmonica for me. Like most shy people, he deeply appreciated my affection and returned it with a happy smile. When he and my mother wanted to be alone, they would give me money to see a movie. Although I enjoyed going to the movies, I used to feel unwanted, rejected and sad, and I resented being sent away by my mother after we had been everything to each other for so many years.

When I was fifteen, they finally got married. I attended the wedding, my second one, but this time with a real live groom and father. It was a small affair with only a few friends and relatives in attendance, but there was plenty of wine flowing and much laughter ringing out. That evening I whispered in his ear "Daddy," and a sunny grin lit up his whole face. I was very happy.

He was trained as a baker, not because he wanted to be a baker but because his father was a baker. In the days of his youth most sons simply followed in their fathers' footsteps without questioning. My stepfather was a fairly intelligent man, and if he had had the opportunity to study, he might have pursued a profession that ultimately might have been more fulfilling. He had a facility with words, and he loved making speeches. He could rant and rave against the government so eloquently that I admired him for it. One of his anti-communist speeches held in his earlier years had excited his audience to the point where they were breaking chairs over each other's heads.

Dare I say it? He was a Nazi. It is not that difficult to imagine the seductiveness of an ideology which suggested to people that they were born into a master race, that they were destined to rule over others without having to earn that right. The less accomplished and the more frustrated a person was, the greater the appeal must have been. My stepfather, like so many others, could not see, and perhaps did not want to know, the horrors which were perpetrated under the auspices of that ideology. At the time when I met him, nobody admitted to having been a Nazi any more, everybody had been "denazified." But not in their hearts. Not even he.

But my stepfather was not an evil man. In the war he was a medic because he preferred healing to killing. He had seen many a young life snuffed out in its prime, and there was one in particular whom he could never forget. Tears welled up in his eyes when he told us the story of young Henlein whose torn-up body he was holding in his arms while the brave soldier sang "So nimm denn meine Haende" ("Take my hands now"), offering his soul to God. I always cried with him when he told me that story.

When he first came to live with us, he worked as a cook for the U.S. Army stationed in Stuttgart, and he would often come home with some leftover food which his employers let him have, tasty morsels which we ate gratefully. Food was still scarce in Germany at that time.

Life was not always easy with my stepfather. There were very few people he was fond of, and I don't recall that he ever had any friends of his own visit him. He adored my mother. He loved me, too, but there were times when my mother gave him reason to be jealous of me. She would not allow him to act like a father with me, to scold me if I was bad or lazy. It must have cut him to the quick when she said to him: "She is not your daughter."

He was fastidious and pedantic, and he could fly into a rage over a matchbox left on the wrong table. His anger was seething just under the surface, ready to flare up at the slightest provocation. We had terrible arguments and shouting matches when I felt wrongly accused by him. I remember one occasion when I became so upset that I started tearing out my own hair. His hair was what I really wanted to tear out, but I didn't dare, of course. I was afraid that he would strike back at me (although he never ever did), and on a deeper level I was afraid of losing him. My mother, too, suffered from his fits of temper and said that he was ruining her nerves. He was a strange man, a sensitive loner, and I often thought that the war was to blame for most of his problems. My mother's friends came to visit less and less, and she who had once been so lively and outgoing became more and more reclusive.

And yet, he would have given his right arm for either one of us. He had been married once before and had a daughter of the same age as myself. While he was away in Russia, his wife betrayed him with another man. His wound was so deep that he could not even bear to see his own daughter again. She would have reminded him too much of her mother. After he died, I found among his belongings a little silver signet ring with her name "Rosemarie" engraved on it. He had it made for his little girl but never sent it to her. Another emotionally charged object which he left behind is a small square bag made of very thick leather. He used to carry it, filled with first aid items, strapped to his belt in battle. He was always very particular with his things, and this bag, I believe, was one of his greatest treasures. After the war he used to keep his razor in it and a few other items for personal grooming. Now, when I hold this bag in my own hands, I can almost feel the pain, the courage, the fear, the horror and the hope of the man who carried it and touched it.

Even though he had not gone to high school, my stepfather encouraged my mother to let me go right up to the "Abitur," the final examination in high school. This meant that they had to provide for me until I was 18 years old, but he realized that the best dowry they could give me was an education. In those days only about 10 percent of students finished high school, and the "Abitur" opened many doors besides the portals of university. I was thrilled and grateful when the decision was made, because I had a great love for learning. One time he gave me an encyclopedia for my birthday, and he wrote inside the cover: "Knowledge is power." Power was what I needed, the natural and easy power which self-confidence bestows. I felt deficient somehow, being fatherless. Most of my friends had fathers, and those who did not, had lost theirs honorably on the battlefield. God only knew where mine was. Like most illegitimate children, I also knew the embarrassment of poverty. Fortunately I did well in school, and the knowledge which I acquired there, as well as the good grades which I received for my work, gave me a certain power without which I would have been a pitiful little waif.

My stepfather was born in Dueren, a town near Cologne, while my mother and I came from Southern Germany. This meant that we spoke almost two different languages. Mother and I found his dialect so much more charming than our own Swabian speech that we used to imitate him and adopt certain words of his into our own language at home. This delighted him. All three of us had a childish sense of humor. Instead of asking me, for instance, if I had dusted the top of the bookcase, he would ask me if I had been to Tibet, and I knew exactly what he meant. Or we would make up funny languages with a useless syllable added to each and every word. I remember times when I laughed so hard that I was rolling on the floor, begging for mercy.

Nowadays he would be called an "audiophile" because he was fanatical about sound, he bought the most expensive stereo equipment he could afford and set up loudspeakers all over the apartment. There was a pair of them on top of "Tibet" that looked like a couple of Greek urns and another one hanging ominously in a corner next to a doorway, a rather ugly piece of machinery which my mother and I would have liked to hide, but he loved it. He also loved birds. They drew out all the tenderness that was in him. His two budgie birds would sit on his head any time they were in the mood, and when he sat down to eat, they would perch on his hand and ask for a bite. They were even allowed to fly freely around the apartment for their recreation, leaving their moist little droppings on the velvety upholstery. They could do no wrong.

As I said before, my stepfather was ambitious for me. He wanted me to study hard and make something out of myself. At 19, when I was already working as a salesgirl and studying shorthand (for business) and philosophy (for fun) in night school, I met a young man who wanted to be my boyfriend. I asked my parents if I might go out with him on a date. They were outraged. How could I possibly think of going out with men? I had a lot of studying to do, and they implied that I had a choice between improving myself and fooling around. They came down hard on me. To this day I do not really know which one of the two was the initiator of this attack, but I strongly suspect that it was my mother who feared that I might become a loose woman. I told the young man no, I was not allowed to date him, but I felt no great regret. His kiss in the moonlight had not ignited my senses— he was obviously not the man of my dreams, or I would have disobeyed my parents' absurd order.

When I visited them years later with my own little baby (a perfectly legitimate baby), my stepfather behaved just like a real flesh-and-blood grandfather with him, cuddling and jostling and teasing my son, delighting in his delight, proud in his small accomplishments. He became my father all over again. And yet… Some part of me could never wholeheartedly accept him as my father. He had not been with me when I had just arrived in this world, had not fondly looked into my unknowing but curious new face, had not let me twist my tiny fingers around his big finger and pressed me against his strong chest. And most of all, his blood did not run in my veins. I held it against him that he was not my real father.

In the end, my poor stepfather was bed-ridden with cancer. When I flew to Germany to visit him in the hospital, my heart sank at the sight of him. Even though he was skin and bones, his feet were swollen to twice their normal size. He was very happy to see me—it was the first time in about two years, and he was still able to talk to me, we even had a few laughs. I remember buying him some beer and he got mad at me because it was canned rather than bottled. I also brought him food which my mother and I had cooked at home, and he savored every morsel of it. The way in which he spoke about his condition ("As soon as I get better…") clearly showed that he did not know, or rather did not want to know, that he was dying.

His doctor insisted that he had to be transferred to a nursing home because there was nothing more that could be done for him at the hospital. I rode with him in the ambulance which transported him to his dying place. Once he was put to bed there, he hardly spoke any more and slept most of the time. The nursing home was a long way from where my mother lived and I knew that it would be difficult for her to find it when she wanted to visit him. So I went along with her and carefully showed her which train to take and which bus to catch. All the while I had a sinking feeling that she would never remember it.

I visited him a couple of times more. Once I took him, all bundled up in a wheelchair, for a walk in the lovely garden which was laid out behind the building. The sun was shining, and there was a strong love between us while a silent farewell was being said. The next time I came to see him, he did not seem to be aware of my presence. I asked the doctor how long he might live, and he said it could be weeks, or it could be months. I had to go back to Canada where my husband and children were waiting for me. All I could do was to ask that they give him all the beer he wanted and that they should not keep him artificially alive.

After my last visit with my stepfather I was terribly shaken and, instead of going straight to the bus stop, I wandered through the garden behind the nursing home. The tears that welled up in my eyes acted like magnifying lenses, and suddenly I could see every blade of grass, every leaf and every flower in finest detail. And there was something else that I saw, or rather knew, at that moment: A man's body may die, but all his experiences, his memories, feelings, thoughts and dreams, all that he was, can never fall into oblivion.

I had five days before flying home to Canada, and I had made arrangements to visit relatives in Austria where I would meet, for the first time ever, my half-sister. Up to this day I am ashamed for having left my poor father to die alone. I should have stayed by his side, no matter who was waiting for me. He died the day after I flew home. In my sorrow, I suddenly felt a strong aversion against wearing jewelry, and I dressed without my usual flair. To me that was a sacrifice (a small one, to be sure) since I am fond of adorning myself. My stepfather's death was the only death which called for that ritual, and I believe now that it was a ritual of atonement, dictated by my feelings of guilt for not having stayed with him at least five more days.

They say that a girl chooses a husband in the image of her father. My husband does indeed have some of my stepfather's qualities. To begin with, there is a physical similarity, if not a resemblance, between the two. And my husband is a very intense man with deep feelings which he carefully shields from anybody's view. He is highly responsible and dependable, loyal and devoted to his family. He, too, is quick to lose his temper over some bagatelle and can cause the whole household to fall into upheaval when he is in a bad mood. Like my stepfather, he is not very sociable but has a great love for animals. He also has a wonderful sense of humor, only his is expressed more in witty remarks than in the childish nonsense that my stepfather used to favor. Both were born under the sign of Virgo. Even though my stepfather entered into my life when I was already 12 years old, he must have helped shape my unconscious image of the ideal man.

As far back as I can remember, my mother used to talk to me about my real father. She never spoke with any bitterness about him, only told me that he and she had gone their separate ways before I was born. Naturally I was filled with curiosity about this mysterious man who was so close to me and yet I could never fly into his arms or show him how I could dance. I knew that he was Austrian, tall and blond with blue, blue eyes which had kept my mother spellbound. I also knew that he had a good singing voice and had some operatic training. During the war he was a combat photographer. The stuff dreams are made of.

I had a fantasy that some day he would come and live with us, and I would have a real family just like all my little friends had. He would find me and be sorry that he had deserted me. Naturally I thought that he was as handsome as a king, as intelligent as a philosopher, and as warm as only a father could be. My mother had a little hand-painted sign tacked to the wall that said "J'attendrai" (I will wait) which was the title of a popular song in the '40s. She waited and she waited... Last year when I participated in a voice workshop, that song suddenly came out of my mouth, and I realized then that it was exactly the same melody as the theme of Madame Butterfly, the woman whose husband abandoned her and her child, the woman who longingly peered down into the harbor every single day for several years awaiting his return. My mother had told me once that she had cried for three days after she saw the opera.

She never stopped loving my father, not when she married the first time, and not when she married the second time. And I believe that for many years she still harbored some irrational hope that he would come back to her. And I, his little daughter, could never accept another man to be completely my father. All my life I longed for the elusive man whose flesh and blood I was, the one with whom I shared so much and yet so little. Once, in a yoga class taught by a man in his late forties, the students were all lying on the floor relaxing, while he went around covering each one of us with a blanket. When he came to me and carefully gathered the blanket around my body, tears suddenly filled my eyes, they came faster and faster, and I just wanted to cry my heart out without knowing why. Only later did I understand that this man, with his small gesture of fatherly kindness, had reminded me of what I never had as a child.

At the age of 21 I moved into my own apartment in order to escape the constant supervision at home. This was an important step in my life and prepared me for the next step: to find my true father. I had no idea where in the world he was, I only knew that his birthplace was the town of Linz on the Danube. In those days everybody's whereabouts were registered with the police department, and this is where I got my answer: I wrote to the police in Linz and could hardly believe my eyes when I held his precious address in my trembling hands. He lived in Venezuela.

I have kept a copy of the letter which I sent to him. I called him "Dear Mr. Kronberger" and reminded him of the time when he met my mother in a cafe in Stuttgart where she served him coffee, cakes and wine. (Her colleagues could tell when he entered the cafe just by the way her eyes began to glitter...) I enclosed some photographs of my mother and myself and told him that I wanted to meet the man whose eyes and nose I had, that I had a great longing to see my biological father. And I assured him that I would make no demands on him except that he reveal himself to me, let me have contact with him. After a brief description of my life I begged him to send me a reply soon and not to let me wait another 21 years.

A month later I held his letter in my hands. "Dear Miss Valentina..." The initial thrill soon gave way to a sense of disappointment. Instead of receiving me with open arms and calling me his long-lost daughter, he talked around the subject with the caution of a cat exploring new territory. He said he could not say for certain that I was not his daughter, but on the other hand he did not have the courage to simply call me his daughter. He said that he admired my courage for writing to him and that I had every right to know who my father was, that I had probably been tortured for many years by the uncertainty, and that this doubt can be an inhibition for a person's whole lifetime. Yes indeed. At least he understood that.

He wondered what he could be to me at this stage of my life. Did I not hate him for having deserted me, could I possibly have any filial feelings for a man I had never seen? Perhaps I had an ideal image of him engraved in my mind which would be wiped out if I met the real man. Despite all these doubts, he promised to come to Germany in the following year, and then we would have our blood tested in order to clarify the situation once and for all.

I was overwhelmed. He would come, He, my father, would come to me, look at me, speak to me, acknowledge my presence and prove our blood relationship. Despite the shadow which his doubt had cast over my soul, I was in heaven.

In my next letter I asked him for a photograph. I needed to know what he looked like, I said, because, who knows, it could happen that we would meet somewhere and I might fall passionately in love with him, not knowing his true identity. What a tragedy that would be. A Greek tragedy. Therefore it was urgent that he send me a photograph of himself. He sent me several, and I loved the way he looked, handsome in a Johnny-Carson-kind-of-way, his masculinity tempered with a certain gentleness and Austrian charm. Simone, his wife, thought my reasoning was very funny and made sure that he included her picture so that I could see who my adversary would be, in case my scenario ever came true.

We kept on corresponding for several years, and while I told him about my move to Canada and my marriage there, he gave me, little by little, a picture of his own life. After he had met (and left) my mother he had attended flying school and had become a trainer of pilots. He also flew supply planes to Russia. About a year after their brief affair he met his wife Simone, a beautiful Belgian woman who was to remain his wife to the very end of his days. Their love was mutual and forever. I could not help wondering what would have happened if he had not met her and had returned to my mother, had seen me, the little baby girl who was a part of him, mind, body and soul. Would he have stayed with us? My heart does somersaults at the thought.

Work was hard to find at the war's end, but Simone had an adventurous uncle in Venezuela who had gone all by himself into the jungle and built himself a ranch there. Surrounded by native Amerindians, he was lonely for people of his own kind, and besides, he needed help to run the ranch. So my father became a cowboy. Ah, what a picture: my father galloping on a tall horse, his sky-blue eyes squinting to shut out the burning sun, his blond hair flying in the wind, as he was driving the lackadaisical cows over the prairies. Simone told me the story of their first visit to the little native village and how the native women invited her to have a bath in the river, how they watched every move she made and couldn't stop giggling when they saw her white skin. My father had a similar experience with the men from the village. After their ritual bath, they were served a sumptuous meal spiked with some questionable ingredients which they did not dare to investigate. The two of them were dining by themselves in an open hut while the whole village watched them eat.

Eventually my father wanted to be his own boss. He and Simone moved to the capital Caracas even though he had no idea what he would do there for a living. They rented a small flat, and he answered an advertisement for an elevator technician. The only experience he had with elevators was going up and down in them, but he was handy with tools and he needed a job desperately. He convinced the employer that he was qualified (in Latin America anything is possible if one has plenty of nerve) and he got the job.

Then he realized that there were many Germans in Caracas who were all homesick and hungry for news from the homeland. His next project was a small shop where he sold German newspapers and magazines. The business grew until eventually he heard of a chance to start a whole new enterprise, a ceramics company in a smaller town called Ciudad Bolivar. After many trials and tribulations he became president of his own company and ran a successful business for several years. My father, the business tycoon. Everything I learned about him added more detail and color to the romantic picture I had painted of him.

At some point my father and I lost contact with each other because we both moved and we had no common connection. I felt as if I had lost a great treasure.

Several years later my husband had to go to Caracas on business. Since we had planned to spend our holidays in Barbados that year, the children and I went along with him so that we could fly there once he finished his work in Venezuela. In Caracas we were booked at the Tamanaco, a beautiful hotel with a huge swimming pool surrounded by little cabanas.

Once installed at the hotel, I began to think that perhaps, by some chance, maybe... my father might be living in Caracas, although his last letter had come to me from Ciudad Bolivar. One never knows what miracles fate can weave. With trembling hands I opened the thick telephone book, my heart already knocking hard against my chest. But there was no Adam Kronberger, no Kronberger at all, not even one called Klaus or Peter. This did not stop me. I knew that many people who have telephones in Latin America are not listed in the telephone book. But what could I do? The Embassy. I would call the German Embassy. "Adam Kronberger?" the girl said, "you mean the one who has the import business on Avenida Cumana?" "Yes, please give me his telephone number!" She did.

When I called, a woman answered, and I asked to speak to Mr.

Kronberger. Later I learned that the woman was Simone, and she told me that when he took the phone, she saw him suddenly turn white. All I did was tell him that I, his daughter, was in town with my husband and our two children, and that I would like to see him. He would come to meet me the next morning at the hotel, he said, at 11 o'clock. There I was, 36 years old and about to meet my father for the first time in my life.

Eleven o'clock is not too early to have champagne, and champagne I ordered, while my heart was trying to jump out of my mouth. I wore a silky blue dress with white polka dots, the most flattering thing I could find, and I combed my hair just so, then put on a little lipstick and powder, for I wanted to please him. At last there came a knock on the door, I flew to open it, there he was. Handsome, wonderful. We were both shy, shook hands and addressed each other in the formal way which was really absurd considering our relationship. He said: "You are so small." I didn't know whether that was a reproach or a compliment, but I decided to take it as the latter because he seemed content with what he saw. He met the children: Christopher, aged six, already understood that this stranger was not really a stranger, and two-year-old Leila flirted a little with him, as was her way. They both liked him, I could tell, and he seemed to like them, too. After all, they were one-fourth his.

We sat down and toasted our meeting with champagne. (I still have the cork!) Then we talked, and we talked and we talked. We decided that we would drop the formal "Sie" in favor of the familiar "Du" and call each other by our Christian names. This form of address was my suggestion because he still had not fully and officially acknowledged our relationship. I would call him "father" later when the moment was right. As we talked with each other, I felt more and more comfortable with him, and it seemed to me that the chair in which I sat was hovering three feet above the ground. We found out that we had many things in common. We both loved good books and classical music, especially Mozart who was his favorite as well as mine! And we both collected reproductions of old Madonna-and-Child paintings. There was a calmness and a wonderful gentleness about him. When he left, he hugged me and the children. Afterwards Christopher said to me:

"Mom, you must really love that man." Children can be so wise.

That evening my husband and I were to meet him and his wife for dinner. I was so enchanted by him that I did not even worry about meeting her but fully assumed that she would be a lovely person, too. And she was. Simone received me with open arms, literally, and she had brought a precious gift for me: a gold wreath pin with pearls and emeralds which my father had once given to her. It was a symbol of reunion, a token of love. The evening was delightful. We dined at an Italian restaurant where the animated conversation flowed in all directions among the four of us. Both my father and Simone spoke fluent English which made it possible for my husband to be included in the foursome. Somewhere in the back of my mind I had the satisfaction of having appeared on my father's doorstep not as a poor orphan begging for help but as a young woman happily surrounded by her family.

The next day we visited my father's shop. He imported beautiful china, crystal and silverware from Europe to sell them to nostalgic Europeans who were longing for a piece of home and to wealthy Venezuelans who appreciated the fine quality of his wares. We left with our arms full of gifts: a copper fondue set, a cuckoo clock from the Black Forest, and a large hand-painted ceramic plate from Austria. In the evening we visited him and Simone at their apartment. I had to remind myself that I was not dreaming but that I was really standing in my father's living room, chatting with his wife and drinking his wine. Simone was a lively, intelligent woman with a great sense of humor and a natural warmth which did not allow any awkward moments to develop between us. I loved her, too. She and my father had never had a child, and Simone said to me, just as we were leaving: "I wish you were my daughter."

A wonderful long letter from my father awaited me at home, a letter in which he actually called himself my *father*. And he said: "You are for me the ideal girl that one could wish for in a daughter. Pretty and intelligent, well bred, and with her heart in the right place." These words remain in my mind.

The following year we passed again through Caracas on our way to Barbados, and when we arrived at the Tamanaco, fifty pink roses were waiting there for me from my father! This time we all met around the swimming pool. He and Simone owned one of the cabanas at this hotel. We were becoming more and more familiar with each other, more and more "related."

I felt it was time to ask about my half-sister. I had always known from rumors that somewhere in Germany there was a young woman who looked very much like me, and that she was also my father's daughter. She was a little older than I—nobody in my family knew who her mother was. My father told me that my sister had come to live with him when she was 18 (he had actually gone to Germany to bring her back—her, not me!), and that she had married an Italian with whom she was now living in a small town in Venezuela. She had two children, just like me. Could I meet her? He was evasive and said I should go slowly in such a delicate matter, because he had not yet told her of my existence. I let it go, determined nevertheless to find her one day since she was also of my blood.

The third time I saw my father was also the last. In all, I have spent no more than 30 hours with him. I never forget the long drive to Maiquetia Airport in his Mercedes which he enjoyed so much. We talked and the stereo was playing popular German music which he had taped which stirred up many emotions in me. Why, oh why had he not married my mother? He said they had serious problems, and one day he would tell me. But he never did, there was no time, and perhaps he did not want to tell me anyway. My mother never told me either. Let it sleep, let *them* sleep.

For the first time in my life I felt whole, complete. I knew who I was. Even my plants grew greener. I was so in love with my father that it never even occurred to me to be angry with him for having deserted me; all I felt was a deep gratitude for having found him, and for being accepted by him. It was my mother whom I blamed for letting him get away.

When I met him for the very first time, I wrote to my parents in my great excitement, describing every detail of the momentous encounter. I thought they would be happy for me, especially since my mother had always encouraged me to find my father. She herself had never made any attempt to find him or ask him for help, but I believe that she wanted to show him that she had managed to bring up his child all by herself.

A reply came from both of them, my stepfather's part signed "Uncle Joseph." They both felt rejected now that I had found my real father, because he was so wonderful and successful and could speak English and had a charming wife! I was angry, sad and disappointed. I wrote them an urgent long letter in which I made it very clear that my feelings for them had not changed one iota, that I loved them as much as ever, and that they were behaving like a couple of children. They understood. Human feelings are so fragile, so easily hurt, especially when there is some reason for insecurity.

My father eventually retired to Austria, his homeland. In his last letter he said that he was looking forward to our visit, and that now he would have time for us, and we would really get to know each other. Oh how I longed to be there. But it never happened. One day I received a telegram from Simone telling me that he had died. Now I *raged*. I was so furious and angry with him that I threw things around the house and called him names. Even my cat hissed at me. So he had *deserted* me once again! I raved until I was totally exhausted. Then I arranged to have white lilies sent to his grave and a ribbon with the words "With love and sorrow…" in gold letters. I never did call him "father."

Several years later I met my half-sister Ursula and her husband at Simone's house. Even though we are two very different personalities, I feel a deep bond with her, and she with me. The family resemblance is obvious, not only between her and me, but even among our children. Sometimes I feel a surge of jealousy at the thought that she was the one my father took into his home and not I, but then I tell myself that it must have been very difficult for him to appear with an 18-year-old illegitimate daughter. To bring yet another one on the scene, one who was merely nine months younger and had a different mother, would have shocked even his most liberal friends!

There were other relatives, too, whom I met for the first time after my father's death. The one I loved most was his brother who took an instant liking to me, and we corresponded for a while. I asked him questions about my father's life, and he told me everything he could remember. He was a little older than my father and had always adored his younger brother. Now he is dead, too. I still visit Simone every now and then and hungrily listen to her stories about the man we both love. He binds us together, but beyond that we are also very fond of each other. She has kept his study intact so that it looks as if he had just walked out the door. His pen set still sits on the desk. Sometimes I linger in there all by myself, drinking in the atmosphere, asking questions of the walls. A large painting of a panther with devil's eyes and fearsome fangs sends shivers down my spine every time I look at it. How foolish to be frightened by a mere picture at my age! But I am spellbound by the message which it seems to convey to me: that my father, angel of light, had a dark side, too. In the few golden hours which we spent together, that part of him had never made an appearance. "Do not idealize me," the panther seems to say. I fondle the wooden candlestick which my father carved and wonder what life would have been like with him at my side.

Permission

Richard Cole

Remember the last time you saw your father,
how he couldn't make words, and you
told him what people said who had
died and returned, how they saw brilliance
at the end of a tunnel, and the feeling
of floating up some sort of ramp...
Remember then how you felt forty years
of anger at a dark, immobile father
slip away and you loved him absolutely
for the few moments before you left.
And remember what seemed like
gratitude in his eyes, as if someone,
without thinking, had finally
given him permission.

Abuelo Cesar Ate With His Fingers

Janice Levy

Whenever we made the trip into Brooklyn it rained or snowed and we'd get stuck in traffic for hours. My mother shivered and blasted the car heater. My father rolled down all four windows and threatened to turn around and drive home because he didn't want to visit her old man, anyway.

"Me, neither," I'd say from the back seat, and then they'd both yell at me. I was ten years old and I didn't like to visit Abuelo Cesar, even if it was only once a month. My grandfather ruined my whole day.

I didn't even like to look at him. Water leaked out of his eyes and he stuck little pieces of tissue all over his face when he cut himself shaving. He smelled like the green soap from the library bathroom. Even in the winter he wore a white short-sleeved shirt with a pocket, the kind my dentist wore. His pants were dirty and he pulled them high over his stomach with a belt that was missing most of its loops. My mother said he looked this way because after *Abuela* Juani died he didn't have anyone to look after him. And the theater where he worked as a custodian had closed down, so he didn't have anything to do. I said it was because he ate with his fingers and wiped his mouth with the back of his hand. And he talked and chewed at the same time, something which I wasn't ever allowed to do. Besides, I didn't even know my grandmother. She died right before I was born. My grandfather never took care of me when I was younger and he hardly ever came to our home.

I didn't like to visit my grandfather. I didn't like his house. There was no backyard, just an alley on either side with tin garbage cans. There were rocks and pebbles in the front of his apartment building instead of flowers. I never saw any kids my age playing outside in the street. *Abuelo* Cesar covered the furniture and the carpeting in the living room with plastic. The sofa and chairs stuck to my legs and made me all sweaty. And there were these candles he lit and little statues around in every room. In the winter when it got dark out early, the whole place looked spooky. I couldn't wait to get home.

My best friend Ashley had a grandfather who was famous. He was a surgeon on the soap opera, "General Hospital." Ashley said he lived in Hollywood and had a swimming pool *in* his living room. He drove a silver Mercedes—the big one. My grandfather didn't know how to drive. That's why my mother brought him chicken and meat from the butcher in brown paper bags that were wet at the bottom and leaked onto the floor. *Abuelo* Cesar tried to stuff money in her hand but she'd push it away. My father would tell her, "You don't wanna insult the old guy," and he'd put the money in his own pocket.

Then we'd sit down in the kitchen. *Abuelo* Cesar drank his coffee black in a little doll's cup. He'd heap in the sugar like he was shoveling snow. To me, the coffee tasted like a brown crayon. *Abuelo* Cesar gave me a yodel and a glass of milk in a green chipped cup on a yellow plate. My mother and grandfather talked in Spanish, so fast that the words sounded like Woody Woodpecker laughing. My father would look at his watch and yawn, "When you gonna learn English, Pops?" Then he'd escape to the living room and turn the ballgame on so loud my mother would have to shout to be heard. My mother translated *Abuelo* Cesar's questions. They were always the same. I would tell him yes, that I was studying and yes, that I was obeying my parents, and no, that I didn't have a boyfriend, yet. He was easier to lie to than my parents.

Since I couldn't understand what they were talking about, I made a big deal out of eating my yodel. I peeled off the outside chocolate and ate that first, picking out the chocolate that stuck under my fingernails. Then I unrolled the yodel, layer by layer, until only the cream was left. I saved that for the end. I put the crumbs in my cup so the milk looked like it had freckles. From time to time, my grandfather would touch my face and smile. His knuckles were bumpy and his hands reminded me of an old baseball mitt, punched out and worn. Ashley's grandfather got manicures and played a baby grand piano. He had never cut sugar cane.

When I was finished eating, I'd sneak out of the kitchen and wander into *Abuelo* Cesar's bedroom. I'd look at the black and white photographs stuck to every inch of space on the walls with yellow tape. Mostly, they were pictures of my grandfather as a young man, on a beach holding up a fish he caught, or on a bicycle with a straw hat. He was barefoot and there was often a pretty woman with long dark hair standing or sitting close behind him.

Then I'd close the bedroom door and touch the statues of the ladies holding crosses. One time I turned them all around so they were facing backwards. I dropped a statue and a blue stone fell out and fell behind the radiator. I hid the statue in the bottom of *Abuelo* Cesar's sock drawer. The next time I was there, the statue was sitting in the same place on top of the radiator. This time it stared at me with one eye. I'd take my sketch pad and pencil and move a wooden chair to the bedroom window. Across the street, the houses were short and dark and looked like little raisin boxes. The branches on the trees looked like my hair when I got up in the morning, tangled with knots. I'd stay at the window and draw until it got dark outside and my father would start to make noise and stomp around the house. *Abuelo* Cesar would kiss me and say, "Dios te bendiga." He never blessed or kissed my father. He never even shook his hand.

On the way home, my mother would cry because *Abuelo* Cesar seemed to be getting so old so fast and he refused to wear his hearing aid. "The old guy will outlive all of us," my father would say as he raised the volume of the car radio, "Besides, it's good to be a little deaf now and then." In the dark, I'd watch my mother wipe her eyes and I'd play tic-tac-toe against myself on the foggy backseat windows.

One time, my parents had a fight at my grandfather's house. My mother wanted *Abuelo* Cesar to live with us because he fell on the ice and forgot to take his heart medicine. He also kept sour milk in the refrigerator.

"Who's gonna watch the old guy when we're both at work?" my father yelled. My mother said that *Abuelo* Cesar could share my room and that when I got home from school, I could watch him.

"I'm not sharing my room with him!" I shouted. Everyone looked at me. For a minute I thought that *Abuelo* Cesar understood what I said because he tilted his head at me like my dog did when I told him to get off the pillow. My father pulled my mother by the arm and I heard the front door shut. *Abuelo* Cesar and I sort of looked around at the ceiling and the floor and finally at each other. He smiled and shrugged his shoulders up so high they touched his ears. He took a glass and filled it with something from a tiny bottle with a shiny label. He winked and passed me the glass. I drank and bit and choked because I felt like I had swallowed a lit match. *Abuelo* Cesar laughed and drank down the liquid in one gulp, just like the cowboys did on TV. Then he grabbed his throat with both hands and pretended to strangle himself. He stuck out his tongue and closed his eyes. *Abuelo* Cesar drank from my glass and pounded his chest with both fists. "Ahh!" he yelled like King Kong. I tried not to laugh, but he really looked silly.

I followed him into the bedroom. He opened up a drawer under his lamp and took out a photograph of the young woman with long dark hair. He pointed to the necklace in the photograph. "Perla," he said. The woman had brown eyes and wasn't smiling.

Abuelo Cesar touched my long dark hair and looked back at the photograph. Then he opened up another drawer and took out a big pad of drawings done in charcoal and colored chalk crayons, the kind you could smudge with your fingers. He flipped the pages quickly, so they looked like a movie. I saw lots of palm trees in different shades of green, a white and black goat, and orange sunsets. He pointed out the window and pretended to draw on his pad. I wanted to ask him if his eyes still saw those things when he looked out his window now.

The next time we visited, my grandfather looked thinner and coughed a lot. My parents went into the living room to call the doctor because my grandfather couldn't remember where he put his pills. He took me into the bedroom and pointed to a jewelry box under his bed. He slid out a pearl necklace from a soft maroon pouch. I felt his rough fingers around my neck. I looked in the mirror. I looked much older.

Suddenly, I heard my parents shouting. *Abuelo* Cesar put his hand on my knee and shook his head. But then I heard the hurting sound and I knew what was happening again. My grandfather must have known, too, because he pulled himself up and we both hurried into the kitchen.

My father stood with his legs spread apart, sucking in air. He ran his hand through his hair and wiped under his nose. My mother sat on a chair with her knees up against her chest. Her head was down and I couldn't see her face. I touched her back. She threw my hand off and stood up.

"Get dressed. We're leaving," my father said in a low voice. He dropped our coats on the floor in front of us. My grandfather grabbed my father's arm and stood so close their chins almost touched. "Te moto, I kill you." I had never heard him speak English before. My father smiled his crazy man smile, the one that made him look like Jack Nicholson.

"Yeah, sure, old man. Anything you say, Pops." Then he turned to my mother and said, "One more minute and your ass is hamburger" and he went out to the car. My mother and grandfather hugged and kissed each other goodbye. This time, I squeezed in the middle between them.

After that, my parents stopped taking me to visit *Abuelo* Cesar. They said that the nursing home doctors wouldn't allow children up to the rooms. I added a rainbow in the sky and a lady with long dark hair to the drawing I had made of my grandfather's block. My mother said *Abuelo* Cesar bragged to all the nurses how talented an artista his granddaughter was.

I showed Ashley my pearl necklace and she said it was real pretty. I decided not to let her borrow it. She had her own grandfather to visit.

Play Me A Song

Joan Hoekstra

My father's thick, stiff fingers smooth a wrinkle in the tablecloth. The skin is soft and pink… the nails are clean and trimmed. The callouses are gone now, but old scars remain.

I wish he could still play me a song. I catch myself drumming a rhythm. I hum a tune inside my head. "Rebecca," that was his song.

"Are you Frieda?" He stares at me, frowning.

"No, Daddy, I'm Joan. I came yesterday. I'll be going home later today. I live in Calgary, remember?"

Still not sure, he stares at me.

"Win was here from Medicine Hat." He says the words with pride.

"She told me she'd been here. I talked to Morris before I left. He'll be coming here next Sunday. More coffee, Dad?"

He nods without answering. I fill the mug and he picks up his spoon and stirs.

"Don't you want cream and sugar?"

"I guess so," he says. He pours from the pitcher. He reaches out again, then hesitates.

His hand moves slow and deliberate, like it did when he used to play chess. But Sunday chess games belong to another time.

He rests his arm back on the table and shakes his head.

"Would you like some sugar, Dad?" I hand him the bowl as I ask. He nods. His lean, angular face looks younger than his eighty-nine years, but his tired eyes are weary of waking.

I stare down at my own hands, my short blunt fingers, my aging skin… I remember us as we used to be.

. . . .

The mandolin looks fragile in the rough square palms that cradle it. Plink... plink... each string is tuned to perfect pitch. The small celluloid pick is barely visible between the thumb and forefinger. How can Daddy move those blunt stubs so accurately on the frets? His hands are better suited to forging horseshoes.

We sit at the kitchen table, doing our homework, Frieda, Winnie, Morris and me. Mamma is busy kneading bread dough into loaves. Daddy sits close to the hot stove.

"I'll take you home again, Kathleen... to where your heart will feel no pain..." My vision of Kathleen is spun in a web of tenderness by the intricate picking of the strings.

"My grandfather's clock was too large for the shelf..." He knows and sings all the verses. "De Camptown ladies sing dis song..." My toes tap do-dah... do-dah. I wallow in the lush spell of lamplight and music.

My father plays "Rebecca."

The coal oil lamp flares briefly as a current of air wafts across the room. The shadows stretch momentarily then settle back to size.

. . . .

"Would you like another cookie, Dad?"

"That would be fine." He sits placidly as I fill a plate from the cookie jar and bring it back to the table.

"I've been meaning to ask you, I'm writing a story and I need to know how much an anvil weighs. I thought maybe you could tell me."

"An anvil? Well... they would weigh... but then..." his voice fades and he frowns as he struggles with the answer.

"I guess I don't remember. I don't remember much lately."

"Do you remember how you built me a play car out of scraps? It had a Clark's soup box for the body, and an old binder seat, a steering wheel..."

"No, I don't remember that."

"But don't you… it had spoke wheels and license plates and Mamma took my picture," I pause.

"I guess… maybe I did that, if you say I did…"

I interrupt. "It's not important." We eat our cookies in silence. He moves crumbs forward on the tablecloth as if moving pawns on a board.

"Do you ever play chess anymore, Dad?"

"Chess?" he says, "No… there's nobody to play with."

There was only one player that ever mattered. Opa… my grandfather.

. . . .

Every Sunday, on our way home from church, we stop at Opa's house. Opa is Mamma's father. Daddy and Opa play chess.

In winter, Frieda, Win, Morris and I go to the attic and read old funny papers. In summer we play outside or walk the mile home.

The women stay in the kitchen, visit in whispers, tiptoe to the living room with steaming cups of coffee, set them quietly next to the players. Neither man looks up.

Mamma talks too much on the way home. She keeps filling the quiet with words. Daddy lost today and won't say anything, no matter how much she tries to coax him.

But it's no better if Opa loses. When Opa wins, he comes for coffee on his way to pick up the mail.

Mamma finally gives up trying to make Daddy talk and stares out the side window of the car. I try to swallow the hard lump that's stuck in my throat.

When we get home, I'm going to find my old doll and color the places where the paint has worn off and the plaster shows through her skin. Then I'll make up a story about her playing piano in Carnegie Hall.

Mamma swears she's going to burn the chessboard.

. . . .

To my father and grandfather, the game was both joy and obsession.

King's rule was law and their Sunday wars continued over thirty years. But as for my mother?

The queen, most valuable piece of the game, was crucial to the battle. She could be captured, replaced by an ambitious pawn... even sacrificed if need be... but queens could not win. The games spilled far beyond the board.

My mother, wife and daughter of embattled kings, was trapped between her loves.

Winning, losing, silence, rage... I learned the rules. When to pretend, when to stay quiet, when to look down, when to hide...

I know how battles were won and lost. I watched and listened until I had the knowin...

Sometimes, even now, I doubt I know my father. Do I see him with my own and not my mother's eyes?

I look at him, sitting across from me, lost in the maze of Alzheimer's. I know he has a secret, hidden in a zone of silence where he exists. A secret he told my mother before they were married and never spoke of again. When he was young, before they left Holland, he found his father hanging from a rope. My father, still a boy, cut him down and saved him from suicide.

I know the family left for Canada in 1910, homesteaded in southeastern Alberta, and within two years drought forced them into tent town on the banks of the South Saskatchewan. Typhoid claimed both his parents on the same night... I know that at fifteen, unable to speak the language, weak from typhoid, my father created his life...

No, I cannot begin to know him.

Checkmate.

I turn to the window, try to hide my face.

"Looks like it's going to be a nice day," I manage to say, "no wind." He takes the napkin I offer and wipes his lips.

He clasps his hands together, closes his eyes and his soft voice recites the closing prayer of his childhood.

"Onze Vader die in de hemel zijte... ," the low murmur rolls smoothly... the ancient Dutch words still fresh and familiar to his tongue.

. . . .

His hands, black with grease, grasp the fruit jar of warm tea I've brought out to the field. The warm wet liquid escapes the rim and lips. He wipes his dripping chin with his dusty sleeve.

He takes his hat off and pounds it against his leg... white forehead crowns a brown leather face. Thick fingers comb through damp hair. With the cotton kerchief he pulls from his pocket, he wipes the band of his hat, his forehead, the back of his neck down the open shirt. The sweat... the dirt... the fruit of hard labor is crumpled into a ball and shoved back into his hip pocket.

Daddy breaks an oatmeal cookie and gives me half. We eat without talking. He hands me the empty jar, puts on his hat and walks the furrow to the tractor.

. . . .

I wash and rinse the lunch dishes, turning them upside down on the drainboard. My father dries and sets them upright, back on the drainboard. He neatly folds the towel and hangs it on the rack.

"I don't know where they're supposed to go." His eyes plead with me to tell him what to do next.

"I'll put them away, don't worry."

"I'm not good for anything anymore." He turns from me and stares out the window. He bends his head, clenches his fists and pounds the counter.

. . . .

Saturday morning has been hot and white heads are building on the clouds in the northwest. They're moving in fast. At noon Daddy and Mamma stand looking at the sky, talking quietly to each other.

Mamma calls us to help put the chickens in the coop while Daddy puts the calves in the barn. Silently, we all go into the house and wait. The kitchen is hot and stuffy, the air incredibly still and heavy.

BANG… the first hailstone falls.

BANG… BANG… BANG…

"Get away from the windows!" Mamma shouts over the noise. We press our backs to the kitchen wall. Morris, hands over ears, squeezes his eyes shut and buries his face against Frieda. Mamma and Daddy don't move from the window. They stand like statues staring… Mamma puts her hand on Daddy's shoulder.

Hail lays waste.

Less than five minutes go by and the sound is gone, only a few intermittent stones, and the sun returns. Daddy, head bent, pounds his fists on the kitchen counter then turns and goes outside. A rush of cold air comes through the open door.

· · · · · · · ·

"Is Mamma lost? She should have been back by now." He searches the crowd of shoppers anxiously.

"She's not lost, Dad. We're a bit early. Come, let's sit over there." I lead him to the chairs located at the store's front checkout. "It just takes her a little longer than it used to. She knows where to meet us."

Cold drafts sweep over my feet as the automatic door opens and closes. Our hands stay clasped. He strokes my arm with his free hand.

"Do you remember how you used to rub my legs when I was little? Mamma said I had growing pains."

He smiles. "All of you had them. Kept Mamma and me busy every winter. Then when we got the furnace… I guess that helped." He lets go of my hand and sits forward, elbows on knees. "You kids all turned out okay anyway."

"Think so?" I grin.

"I think so, Joanie," he pauses. "Do you still play the piano like you used to?"

He remembers who I am, who I was… calls me by name… my voice is husky as I answer. "Not as much as I'd like to."

"That's too bad. I guess you're pretty busy, though. How's your business going?"

"I have my share of problems, but on the whole, it pays my way. Business is no different than farming, good years and bad, ups and downs… "

. . . .

Once in a while, Daddy lets me sit on his lap in church. Then I'm as big as everyone else. He holds the hymn book so I can see… just as if I could read the words and notes. His rich low voice resonates in perfect harmony with the congregation.

He points out the bass notes and I hear his voice go up and down with the moving finger.

. . . .

"I still don't see how you managed to do it." My father shakes his head.

"Do what?"

"Start and run a business all on your own."

"All on my own? Being your daughter had nothing to do with it?"

"No." He pauses and turns to me, "I am proud of you."

I cannot speak.

He looks away, searching the crowd. "You're sure Mamma can find us? She's been gone a long time."

"Before I leave tonight, when we get back to the house, would you play 'Rebecca' on the mandolin for me?"

"Where are you going?" he says. "Don't you live here?"

I take his hand in mine and stroke his thick, stiff fingers. "You can play and we'll sing all the old songs… "

Portrait of a Lawyer as a Young Dad

Janet Hutchinson

This year my father survived a heart attack. It was the spectacular heart-stopping kind and he lived, in part because highly trained, cool and efficient people zapped him with jumper cables, and in part because he never learned how to give up. He was lucky on two counts. He came back to life, and he had a great new story.

"I thought I was in heaven. First, an angel, all dressed in white, was floating over me. Then she was sitting on top of me, beating her tiny fists on my chest and calling my name. Well, if this was heaven I wanted to make a good impression so I said 'hello.' When I did, she just smiled and then climbed down beside me." He pauses here to collect himself, and wait for his audience to catch up. "Turns out she was a nurse doing CPR, and I was back again."

When he grins that lovable lopsided grin he developed as an only child who could do no wrong, I have to laugh. How can you get mad at a man who has just risen from the dead? Believe me, you can. I was amazed at how angry I got when I faced the prospect of going on without him; he had already made it through so much I was beginning to think he was invincible. Just because I know everybody has to die (after all I am a relatively sane grown-up person) that does not mean I am ready to let go of *my* dad. Not only do I love him and I would miss him, but, perhaps more importantly in the long run, who would make me feel special, who would make me laugh?

"They're making me take rat poison." This is the bait. I know it's not true; the medication they are giving him to dissolve the clot still lodged in his heart may be similar to real rat poison but it is not the same; it is significantly milder. Even so, I bite. "Oh, yah?" I say, and wait to see what will come next. He pauses and shrugs. "I've got a couple of guys keeping an eye on my doctor. If it looks like he's hanging around your mother too much, like maybe he's looking for a rich widow, I'm not taking any more rat poison, that's for sure." I can almost hear the rim shot the drummer would give him in vaudeville to punctuate the punchline.

Over the years we have known each other we have both changed. Have we grown and matured? I don't know. Dad is a lot more laid back now and has become a pillar of the community he served so well both on city council and as mayor. At the same time he is still a bratty little boy who takes a sophomoric delight in signing his notes to me, your loving P.F. It is part of a running joke that since he only has my mother's word that he is my father, that makes him my putative father.

After 35 years as a small-town lawyer practicing family law, Dad knows just about everybody in town; he knows where the bodies are buried, which closets hold skeletons and, though strictly second hand, he swears, which bedroom ceilings are cracked. He jokes that just because everybody else has died doesn't mean he will; in fact, he says, he might just decide to go on forever if he's having a good time. He has pushed his luck pretty hard already, this being the second time he has crossed the line, twice too many for my taste.

The first came shortly after he thought that the blood he was passing was a sign of the final stages of advanced stomach cancer. Since it was surely going to kill him, he decided the best course of action was to keep the bad news to himself as long as possible. Planning to be stoic to the bitter end, he began to work as hard as he could; his plan was to make as much money as he could in the short time he felt he had left; he wanted to provide for the widow and orphans he would leave behind. Instead of worrying anybody about his "cancer," he just worked hard, was noble, and took aspirins for the pain.

He was sometimes irritable, difficult to get along with, moody and quick to snap sometimes out of the blue at the noises made by two rambunctious girls and their rowdy friends. He was tired. Since the ailment was an ulcer, the combination of aspirins, stress, and long hours at the office did far more harm than good. Eventually my mother came home for lunch one day to find him on the basement floor hemorrhaging, lying in a pool of blood.

She says that for a split second she was terrified to leave him because she didn't want him to die alone, but she did because she knew she had to call an ambulance, and fast. When the ambulance got to the local hospital, the doctor on duty took one look, jumped in and ordered the driver on to London with the words, "Oh my God! Go! Go! He'll just die here!" and off they went again.

He is one tough buzzard. Perhaps it helped that he was raised in the Great Canadian North: "My childhood in the wildwood" he says. Having Joe Murray as a role model no doubt had a hand in shaping him too. After all, Joe had been mauled and crushed by a bear, had crawled through the woods bloodied and beaten to the edge of town, delirious and too weak to go further; Joe had survived. I have no idea where the fount of determination comes from, to live no matter what. Dad has it, and as a child I was always in awe of him. Surviving this brush with death just added to the mystique.

As a child I didn't understand him, nor did he understand me. The connection came later, and much later we finally came to appreciate each other. I'm glad we took the time, and I'm equally glad that we had the time. Well as I know him, though, he can still catch me napping and get me with a verbal one-two sucker punch.

"I saw that light they talk about shimmering at the end of the tunnel," he said. He was recuperating at home and was bored. Knowing I was going through a phase where I was wondering about reincarnation, religion and life after death he said very seriously, "I saw a pool of shimmering white light at the end of a long dark tunnel, just like they say, and there were people behind the light calling to me." I was amazed. My father had been through an actual after-life out-of-body experience.

With eyes no doubt as big as saucers, I encouraged him to tell all. In the back of my mind was the sure knowledge that my father would never lie to me, or anybody else for that matter. This was no *National Enquirer* story; if *my father* had died and come back then the *Globe* and *Mail* could publish it on the front page as the gospel truth. That was the kind of confidence in him I always had, and still have.

"Yes," he continued gravely, "you know when you die that the doctor opens your left eye and shines a flashlight in just to make sure you're gone? Everybody in the operating room looks over his shoulder to see if you are dead or not, and they all call your name. The light is so irritating that if there's any life in you at all you just want to get up and kill the person shining it in your eye. I know, 'cause it happened to me."

Kaboom! The punch line; a sucker punch. I had fallen hook, line and sinker, and could only laugh. I laughed, Dad laughed, I laughed more because he was laughing; soon we were both paralyzed by the gasping laughter that renders you helpless to move, and finally even to breathe. He was tickled pink to have tricked me, and I was glad that he was still alive to try.

The beauty of the story is that if it is not true, it could be. After all, he did die, and they do shine that light in your eye, everybody knows that. Even if he strung it together in the recovery room, it is still a good story. He claims the first thing he heard was the doctor saying to his nurse, "Well, look at that! You better call my wife and tell her I'll be late for dinner," which Dad took to mean that the doctor had written him off, but was now prepared to sew him back together.

Some of my most vivid childhood memories are of those times I was with my father, perhaps because they were relatively rare, or perhaps because my father was so witty, funny and charismatic that time with him was unlike time with anybody else. One day when I was six my father announced he intended to take a day off work so the two of us could go to Toronto together. I had a pink and white gingham dress with little tiny checks, patch pockets, a crinoline to hold the skirt out full and a white lace peter pan collar. It may have been bought for the occasion because I remember telling my dentist, "My daddy is taking me to Toronto and I'm going to wear a party dress."

After a sleepless night and much fussing and preening on my part we headed out the door early one weekday morning. Since my grandfather was a railroad man, station agent and telegrapher, my father had lived in a train station when he was little. Trains had figured prominently in his childhood, and consequently, there were trains in many of my favorite bedtime stories about when he was a little boy.

Actually going on a train was the most exciting thing that had ever happened to me in the entire six years of my life. I can still remember standing very primly on the platform holding my daddy's hand and watching for the train. Suddenly a great huge train, single headlight a blindingly bright white, roared around the bend. It came closer and closer before finally whooshing past and screeching, cold metal against hot, to a smoking stop, the passenger car right in front of us.

My grandparents always arrived by train when they came to visit so I was no stranger to the procedure that followed. The conductor got out and placed a box on the platform where it became the bottom step of the short flight up to the waiting coach. The new part was getting to step onto the box myself. I eagerly moved forward on six-year-old legs only to discover they were too short to reach the next riser. My father, laughing at my excitement, tucked his broad hands under my arms from behind, scooped me up and set me gently on the top step where the waiting conductor checked our tickets and ushered us to our seats.

The entire day, from that exhilarating moment to the temperature of the summer air and every detail until the car ride home from the station that night, is engraved on my memory. Later he took my baby sister to Toronto too and took her to different places which made my trip even more special because I knew for certain that it had been just for me.

We started by going to the top of the tallest building in Toronto. Today it is dwarfed by its neighbors, but at the time it was the top of the world. We rode up in a special high-speed elevator and my ears popped for the first time in my life. On the roof I was startled and a little embarrassed when I had to hold my full skirt and scratchy crinoline down against the updraft and wind, but the view was thrilling and I soon gave in to the impulse to shout from the highest heights.

We had lunch in the original Imperial Ball Room at the Royal York Hotel. Dad looked dashing in his cravat and white shirt, blue blazer and grey flannels. He says the maitre d' discreetly took him aside and told him, before we entered the nearly deserted ballroom, that a tie was required. A few words were exchanged, and the maitre d' said that he supposed the cravat would be acceptable, provided we didn't dance.

A huge pink "Shirley Temple" cocktail was set in front of me. The bartender had filled a fishbowl glass with a generous jigger of grenadine, at least half a bottle of maraschino cherries and had topped the whole thing with a paper and bamboo umbrella. Following that came two lamb chops, peas, mashed potatoes, and, according to my father, four waiters, who hovered over me cutting my meat and tucking a napkin over my party dress. Dessert was my choice of anything in the three-tiered display of glorious confections which had been wheeled to our table. It was a storybook lunch and, except for the waiters, I had my father all to myself.

The very first time I remember being alone with Dad was the day my sister was born. I was 2½ years old; not old enough to be allowed into the hospital, but Mom missed me and convinced Dad to drive me up to London. He parked the car outside her window and we waved back and forth to each other. Dad and my Gra'ma alternated between going in to visit Mom and the baby and staying out to take care of me. When Dad was with me, we walked hand in hand up and down the block. He taught me to sing a song which went, "I will give you the key to my heart, promise me that we'll never part, madam, will you walk, madam, will you talk, madam will you walk and talk with me."

He loved to sing, and taught my sister and me a lot of songs, crazy songs like "Bloop Bleep" and "Cement Mixer," which he pronounced Sea-ment mixer. I sang one of his songs in grade one as an audition for the choir, only to be told by the music teacher that she thought it would probably be best if I gave up singing altogether. I was devastated; it was years before I figured out the problem. I had sung my song just the way I had been taught by my father, who may have had good intentions but also had a tin ear; he couldn't carry a tune to save his life and I had sung precisely as he did: off key.

Dad was and is a tall, dark, and handsome, charismatic man. Even after Multiple Sclerosis confined him to a wheelchair, the legal secretaries still voted him Woodstock's sexiest man. He laughs at his own expense when he tells the story of one of his clients who, in an effort to ensure he still felt like a real man even though he was in a wheelchair, offered to tell everybody the baby she was carrying was really his, "or at least I will if it turns out to be white," she said.

Just the other day I overheard him telling a friend about his early years as a father. He had come to tuck me in for the night and couldn't find me. "I thought she might have been confused. We had just switched the baby into the crib, and her into a double bed in what used to be the nursery." He found my sister safe and sound in the crib; I was nowhere to be found. He kept looking through the house in widening circles until, led by the sound of a tin trumpet, he found me sitting on the front steps in my nightgown. "I heard a 'Bleeet!' come out of the trumpet," he said, "and a little voice called out 'God, you-hoo! God, are you there?' There was another 'Bleeet' and then the little voice explaining 'God, I just wanted you to know; I'm in a big bed now.'" When I heard him telling that story I was reminded that, while I may not have known at the time, I know now that he always thought I was special and funny; I like that he tells stories about me when I was a little girl.

Fifteen years ago a chubby man in a black bikini, ten-gallon hat and cowboy boots told me my father loved me. Perhaps I should have known, but until then there had always been a distance, a formality, between us as father and daughter. If the truth be known, I was a little intimidated by him.

I was in Florida with my boyfriend. For lack of anything better to do on a sleepy evening in Boca Raton, we drove a little further down the coast to visit one of my father's clients. Since he was also a social friend of my parents in the summer when he and his wife lived in Woodstock, I had no qualms about walking up and knocking on the front door.

The door opened and I started to introduce myself. I gave up on about the fourth syllable and followed my rapidly retreating host into the hall. From there he headed into the dining room where I watched in amazement as he sat down and proceeded to continue eating the meal we had interrupted. For lack of anything better to do, we sat at the table too. We didn't want to interrupt him, and since we hadn't been even vaguely acknowledged, we watched him eat and waited to see what would happen next.

Eventually, when a woman came into the room, we stood up and introduced ourselves to her. In the middle of the pleasantries, hat off but still wearing the boots and bathing suit, our host leapt to his feet, bellowed "I thought you were my wife's new tennis partner," grabbed my hand and looked at my face from about six inches away. "Oh my God! So you're the kid I've heard so much about. Why didn't you say so! We need champagne!"

As we sipped, he proceeded to tell us some stories my father had told him. They were all about me, but not about poor grades, or my not being able to drive a car properly or being too fat. He had a vast store of anecdotes about me doing funny, smart, wonderful things. Through him I heard my father's voice; Dad's unique style of telling a story. There was no question the anecdotes had been memorized as the result of Dad telling and retelling them at cocktail parties and around dinner tables.

I was dumbfounded. I never really knew before that moment how much my father loved me. For almost 20 years I had felt that I should have been a better kid, smarter, funnier, thinner, just better all around. All of a sudden a stranger was telling me stories about myself which were laced with love, affection, pride and admiration. My father had told a stranger what he had never told me.

By the time we got home I'd had time to think and I was angry. "Why didn't you ever tell me you loved me, why did I have to find out from a stranger?" I shouted at the startled man. He replied, amazed, "I thought you knew," and we cried. We went through a whole box of tissues that night, and more later. I began to wonder what other gems were locked in the inaccurate memory of a little girl and we began to talk for the first time, sorting through the misunderstandings from my childhood which had led to the armed standoff of my adolescence.

I told him what I remembered, and he told me his side. There are things we both wish we had done differently. There are things I wish he had said sooner; things I could have said sooner too. Being Dad's daughter has not always been easy; being my father was no day at the beach either. From that point, one I didn't know could be reached by parents and their offspring, honest communication between adults has prevailed and we continue to get to know each other, both as individuals and family members.

My Father's Neck

. . . .

Robert Bly

Your chest, hospital gown
Awry, looks
Girlish today.
It is your bluish
Reptile neck
That has known weather.
I said to you, "Are
you ready to die?"
"I am," you said,
"It's too boring
Around here." He has in mind
Some other place
Less boring. "He's
Not ready to go,"
The Doctor said.
There must have been
A fire that nearly
Blew out, or a large
Soul, inadequately
Feathered, that became
Cold and angered.
Some four-year-old boy
In you, chilled by your
Mother, misprized
By your father, said,

"I will defy, I will
Win anyway, I
Will show them."
When Alice's well-
Off sister offered to
Take your two boys
During the Depression,
You said it again.
Now you speak aptly
Defiant words to death.
This four-year-old—
Old man in you does as
He likes: he likes
To stay alive.
Through him you
Get revenge,
Persist, endure,
Overlive, overwhelm,
Get on top.
You gave me
This, and I do
Not refuse it.
It is
In me.

Send Flowers To The Nurses

Nancy Robertson

I watch Dad in the hospital. "Those damn nurses aren't going to make me do what I don't want to. They aren't going to get away with this. God damn." He struggles against the Mae West that holds him in bed. He throws aside the blankets. "God damn, let me out of here. Bring me my clothes. I'm going home."

"You can't, dear," says Mom.

"Damn you, you're on their side. You don't want me at home. Go to hell then."

"There's no need for that kind of talk," she says.

"I'll talk any Goddamn way I want to."

Why are you swearing? You didn't swear when we spilled our milk, broke the best china, chipped the ivory piano keys with the pliers. Now you're like a frightened bird, caught in the house, smashing from window to window.

· · · · · · · ·

Dad is in his wheelchair when I arrive the next day. His meal tray is still in front of him. He is alone in the room. The other men eat their meals together in the lounge. Dad will not join them.

"Oh, good," I say, as I bend over to kiss him, "you had strawberries for lunch."

"Yes, but they're sure tight on the good food."

"I'll bring you a clean housecoat tomorrow."

"Don't worry about it."

No, I won't worry about it. And you won't worry about it. You will just be an old man sitting in a wheelchair, tied in so you can't fall out and hurt yourself, dozing most of the day with your chin resting on the bright red stains that alarm other visitors to the ward. They don't know anything about you. They look at you with curiosity or fear and quickly look away. They don't know that your appearance was always impeccable. That you went on a picnic with white shirt and tie. That Mom always took along a table-cloth, glass plates and silverware just for you. And a cushion to sit on so you wouldn't get your suit pants dirty. She wore her oldest made-over clothes, her gardening shoes and lopsided hat. She picked berries or looked for pussy willows while you sat and read the paper.

You were always immaculate and tidy. Your hair never grew over your ears, your whiskers never left a shadow on your face, your pens and pen-cils were placed neatly on your smoking stand beside your chair in the liv-ing room. You used ironed cloth handkerchiefs, wore polished leather shoes, drove a washed and waxed car. Now you sit, old and frail, stained and whiskered. I try not to ask, "How are you?" because you look at me and sometimes you tell me. Then I don't know what to say. I hold your hand, or rub your arm. I wish I hadn't asked.

I was about seven when I had my tonsils out. You took me to the hos-pital on your way to work. You picked me up after work. You held my hand and asked me if I wanted to go home the high road or the low road. But my throat hurt too much to sing with you.

· · · · · · · ·

It's 3:30 before I get to the hospital. I sit with Dad for an hour. He's good today. He reads MacLean's. I look through the Daily News. I search the news, the editorials, about town, the want ads and horoscopes. I don't know what I am looking for and I don't find it. No new dimension or direc-tion. No light turned on in a dark room.

I don't think Dad finds any illumination in MacLean's either. He's too tired to look. Doesn't even talk about going home.

He asks me to check to see if Mom's signed her will. He tells me his papers are in order, the house is paid for, he's left lots of money for Mom, and when she goes, it comes to us kids.

"We don't care about the money, Dad."

"Yes," he says, "but I do."

You always cared about money. I was the youngest child, and the only girl. You sat on the edge of my bed when you came to say goodnight, and told me that when you won the Irish Sweepstake, you were taking Mom and me on a trip to Denmark. When I was older, you took me to the horse races and bet on all the long shots.

But with the four boys you set the example. You went to work every morning and came home for supper on time. On paydays you counted the money by tens onto the kitchen table for Mom. She was responsible for the housekeeping on whatever amount you gave her. You looked after the finances. You paid the bills.

When your sons grew up you were so proud of them. Their success was your success. You wore their promotions and accomplishments with shoulders back and chin up.

. . . .

I take Mom to see Dad. He says everything hurts. His hands, feet, legs, back. I'm sure he has sores that we can't see. He's confused. Doesn't know where he is. We wheel him out of his room, down the hallway, into the lounge so he can watch TV.

"You've done a good job redecorating the living room, dear."

She's annoyed with him. Annoyed that he doesn't recognize where he is. She argues with him. "You're not at home."

He smiles sweetly, "I'm not going to bed early tonight. I'm going to wait and go to bed with you."

That night he fights the nurses. "Leave me alone, Goddamn it. Don't touch me. I'm waiting for Mom." He struggles so hard he tips the wheelchair over.

When I see him the next day, the bars are up and he is tied into bed.

A bandage rings his head.

"I feel like such a damn nuisance."

"It's OK, Dad."

"I'm ready to go," he says, "I'm ready. Everything is looked after." His chin quivers. "You take care of Mom. Make sure she gets my Canada Pension."

"I will, Dad."

"I know you will. And the supplement. Don't forget the supplement."

"I won't forget. I think I'll phone the boys tonight."

"No," he says, "let them phone you."

"But they don't know."

"Yes, they know. They will come when it's too late."

He tells me to go home. "Your life is with Bill. Don't feel bad about me. Mom and I have had fifty-seven years together."

I don't want to leave. You saw me through some hard times. You traveled a thousand miles by Greyhound to be with me when I went to court for my divorce, you were not judgmental, you were just there. We drove that thousand miles back together in my blue Pontiac with my two kids. You gave me a home until I found an apartment and a job, you took your grandson to nursery school and picked him up two hours later. You took them both to swimming lessons every Friday. You drew and painted with them at the kitchen table and taught them how to play checkers and gin rummy.

· · · · · · · ·

I take the clippers, scissors and comb with me today. Wheel him into the middle of the room.

"Thanks," he says, "I need a trim."

I place the old sheet over his head. The sheet with the hole cut out of the center. As I cut his hair, the other old men on the ward join us in their wheelchairs. We form a circle. My hands are the only movement. The scissors the only noise. When I finish Dad's haircut, I ask, "Anyone else?"

"Me," says one old guy.

I take the sheet off Dad's shoulders and place it over the man's head. "No," says Dad, "you came to see me."

"I know, Dad, but this won't take long."

"I won't have it. Get me away from here."

I wheel him back beside his bed. "I won't be long," I say.

He often complains about the other men. Says how rude and noisy they are. The man across the room beats the wall with his cane when he needs a nurse, instead of ringing the buzzer clipped to his sheet.

You were always decent, but you were never a prude. You took my youngest brother, Dave, and me to our first evening movie, Picnic. William Holden and Kim Novak. I can still remember it. I must have been about nine or ten. It didn't take you long to realize the subject matter wasn't the same as a Saturday afternoon matinee. You stood up and told us we were leaving, but Dave and I pleaded with you. You sat back down and watched the movie with us.

· · · · · · · ·

My eldest brother phones. "I'm arriving on the evening flight. How's Dad?"

"Not too good. I'm glad you're coming. I'll pick you up at the airport."

I visit Dad in the afternoon. A nurse is setting up the oxygen. Arranging the tubes around his head.

"He's not with us today," she says.

I lean over the bars and kiss him on the cheek. "Hi, Dad."

His eyes focus on my face. He smiles. "Hi, honey."

I tell him the news of the visit. "I'll bring Vince to see you as soon as he arrives."

"He's already been here. He came this morning."

"I don't think so, Dad. His plane arrives after supper. I told him I'd pick him up."

"He's already been here. He was here the same time as Brian Mulroney and Vander Zalm. Mulroney and Vander Zalm were as drunk as lords."

Dad has never liked Brian Mulroney and he has been mad at Vander Zalm for years. "We need more men like Trudeau," he'd tell me whenever we discussed politics.

Mom is going to be mad at Dad. "Don't talk silly," she'll say. But I sit and agree with him as he rambles on about his world as he sees it today.

I feel bad that my brother is going to see you like this. You were always stable. Sensible. Sober. You weren't a drinking man. When my brother, Gerry, returned from his trip to Europe with a bottle of champagne from France, Mom brought out the Danish crystal and placed nine glasses around the dining room table that was set with one of your mother's finest Danish linens. My grandparents were also there for dinner. We all sat around the table and watched you cut the roast paper-thin. The plates were stacked in front of you and you dished up the meat for each of us. When we were all served, you opened and poured the champagne. Dave and I were given the same as the others even though we were barely teenagers. You raised your glass and gave a toast in celebration of your son's return.

. . . .

At the airport, I suggest to Vince that we go for a beer. Somehow I want to cushion the news about Dad. When we get to the hospital Mom is already there.

"I don't know what's the matter with him. He's just not himself." She looks scared. Not mad.

I lean over and take Dad's hand. I give his shoulder a little shake. "Hi, Dad. Look who's come to see you."

I point to the other side of the bed. His eyes follow mine.

"Hello, Dad," my brother says. "How are you?"

"I'm fine, Vince," he answers groggily. "How good of you to come and see me. How's the family?"

"Everyone's fine. They send their love."

"You tell them I love them." He closes his eyes. After a while we hear a light snore. My brother doesn't want to leave him. Thinks he might go at any time.

When I was a young girl you took me to the cafe every Sunday. You told me I could have either a comic book or a chocolate bar. I sat on the floor looking through my favorite comics, then through the glass cabinet that held the sweets, agonizing over my choice. You never rushed my decision. You sat on a stool and had a cup of coffee and a smoke.

· · · · · · · ·

I hear his hollering as I step off the elevator. "Mom! MOM! M-O-O-O-M! Come here! Where the hell are you? Come here right now!"

As I enter the room he asks, "Where's Mom? Everyone's waiting. See? There's Mike and Kathy. Oh, look! Melissa and Shelley are with them." His face is flushed, his eyes bright. His smile crinkles his eyes, his heels shuffle back and forth under the sheet. His arm reaches toward the ceiling and he shakes his son's hand. He walks over to Kathy, puts out his hand, "How wonderful to see you."

He greets them all. Every member of his family including the latest great grandchild. He remembers every name as they appear for him on the ceiling of the Extended Care Ward. He moves his legs as he crosses streets, goes down sidewalks. He shakes hands, admires new homes, teases the youngsters.

He is so busy, he doesn't notice Mom arrive. She doesn't stay. She can't bear to see him like this.

"He has always been a gentleman," she says. "He would never make a scene. He would never raise his voice. I don't want to remember him this way."

But I stay with him until he settles back in the bed.

"Did you have a good time?" he asks.

"Yes," I say. "Did you?"

"I had a wonderful time."

Yes, you always enjoyed your family. You and Mom traveled every

September to visit each of us. You welcomed in-laws and grandchildren without reservation. Mom sometimes suggested going to the Queen Charlottes or taking an Alaskan cruise. But you just wanted to visit your adult children. You always said you were a lucky man to have such a family.

. . . .

I sit on the chair beside Dad's bed. My arms lean on the bars that hold him in like a crib. I rest my head on my arms. It's been a long day. I don't think he knows I'm here but I don't want to leave him. The only noise in the room is the sputtering from the oxygen on the wall. The tube drapes gracefully from the wall to the bed where it rests along the sheets, pillow and finally Dad's head where it looks like he's wearing headphones for a ghetto blaster, except the small plugs are in his nose, not his ears. He is not fighting. Not even with the intravenous needle taped to the top of his hand.

I'm scared to touch him in case I hurt him. His thin arms lie outside the sheets, his elbows and hands bumpy and twisted from the arthritis that has plagued him for years.

I have to go to the bathroom. I'm hungry. I'm stiff from sitting so long. I'm tired. Yet something keeps me here, searching his face. I'm sitting here like an outsider when inside I'm standing on tiptoes, peeking over, trying to see something. I know if I leave, I may not find it.

He opens his eyes. I see his hand tremble as he attempts to lift it from the sheet. I reach between the bars and hold his hand, gently. The skin feels like tissue paper but there is pressure from his fingers as he turns his hand, palm to palm, with mine.

"I love you, Dad."

"I know," he says. "I love you too, honey." His words are slow, his voice weak. "Telegraph the boys. And please send flowers to the nurses."

His eyes close, his hand relaxes. His life is over. One tear escapes and slowly slips down his cheek.

I sit with my hand in his until I can't stand the stiffness in my arms and back any longer. The chair is hard and the position awkward. My arms and shoulders hurt where the metal bars press into me. And I have to go to the bathroom. I can't wait any longer. I can't wait to use the public washroom downstairs. I use the one in Dad's room and hope that no one comes into the room while I'm using his bathroom.

I walk to the nursing station. Then I walk home. My eyes fill up and tears spill down my face. Rain runs off my hat, down my cheeks, drips from my chin and makes my collar wet. I feel the dampness spreading to my shoulders. Wet pants cling to my thighs.

I have a hot bath when I get home. My legs are cold and red and sting when they hit the hot water. I lie back in the tub and hold up my hands. The skin is getting slack now with lines at the wrists and tiny wrinkles like cross-stitch across the front.

I think of him polishing our shoes every Saturday night, teaching us to play ping-pong, and how he could add columns of figures in his head and come up with the correct answer while we were still adding one column at a time, carrying forward to the next row. And when he came home from work how he would sneak up behind Mom, put his arms around her waist and give her a loud smack on the back of the neck.

"No, dear, not now," she'd complain as she stirred the gravy or salted the potatoes. He'd turn and wink at us kids.

The phone rings. It stops after the sixth ring. I climb out of the tub, dry myself and put on a warm housecoat.

"Better get busy," I think.

He would expect me to do things right.

Contributors

Mary M. Alward

I am an Ontario housewife with a grown daughter. For the past two years, I have enrolled in a course with The Writing School in Ottawa. In October 1989, I had an article published in *True Story*. My lifetime dream has been to become a published author of children's books. In the meantime, I have written many works including poetry and short stories. Since the death of my father, "Daddy's Chair" has been in the back of my mind. "Buddies" is the story of the loving relationship I had with my grandfather.

Elisabeth Spaude Aubrey

I am at times bookkeeper, camp-cook, farmer and lookout person on a forestry fire lookout. Writing is something I have done all my life–poems, stories and long involved letters to my grown children. When I heard Dr. Verny on CBC, memories of my father came flooding back, in particular the words, "There is nothing wrong with being afraid.

Valentina Bek

Over the years I have had some articles published in various newsletters, but my preoccupation with writing is mostly of a very different nature. As a graphologist I look at other people's writing and analyze not what they have written but how they have written it. I also have a part-time secretarial job which keeps me in touch with real-life people.

Robert Bly

Robert Bly's poetry has won many awards, including the Guggenheim Fellowship, Ford Foundation Grant, Fulbright Fellowship and National Book Award. His first full-length book of prose, *Iron John*, was an international best-seller. His latest book, *The Rag and Bone Shop of the Heart*, is an anthology of poems for men jointly edited with James Hillman and Michael Meade.

Richard Cole

Richard Cole is the author of *The Glass Children*, a volume of poems published by the University of Georgia Press. His poems have been recognized with various awards and grants, as well as an NEA Fellowship. He works full-time as a technical copywriter in New York City.

Sandra Collier

Sandra Collier is a psychotherapist in Toronto, Canada. She also designs gardens. "My Father's Gold Tooth" is her first published story.

C.B. Follett

C.B. Follett's poems have appeared in several magazines and anthologies, among them Green Fuse, *The Village Idiot, The Dallas Review, The Taos Review, South Coast Poetry Review, Verve,* and *Echoes.* She has also received Second Prize and publication in *The Climbing Art,* and Honorable Mentions and publication in *Iowa Woman,* and *Nostalgia.* She was finalist in the 1992 Writer's Voice award, and has been nominated for a 1993 Pushcart Poetry Prize.

In her other life, she is designer/owner of The Peaceable Kingdom, a ceramic company making animal-related jewelry and sculptures. CB Follett lives in Sausalito, California, perched between the coastal range and San Francisco Bay.

Maria Mazziotti Gillan

Maria Mazziotti Gillan is the author of *Where I Come From: Poems - Selected and New, Taking Back My Name, The Weather of Old Seasons, Flowers From The Tree of Night* and *Winter Light.*

Charlotte C. Gordon

Charlotte C. Gordon is a poet who lives in Gloucester, Massachusetts. She received her MA from Boston University where she studied with Derek Walcott and Robert Pinsky. She received her BA from Harvard/Radcliffe College. Her work has appeared in *Kalliope* and *Riverrun.* Currently, she is a teacher at The Waring School in Beverly, Massachusetts.

Mark Greenside
Mark Greenside has published in many journals and has been awarded many writing residencies. He teaches at Vista College in Berkeley, California.

Joan Hoekstra
Enrolling in a creative writing course at age 51 changed and enriched my career as mother, grandmother and denturist. In addition to operating my own dental clinic, I attend writing workshops and have a novel-in-progress. My work has been published in *Other Voices, Edges* and *Freefall.*

   Being a latecomer to prose and poetry, my source material ranges from a childhood in the small farming community of Monarch, to life as a single business woman in metropolitan Calgary. Rhythms of the prairie landscape are a recurring theme.

Janet Hutchinson
Janet Hutchinson is a Canadian currently living in Halifax, Nova Scotia. The work included in this anthology, "Portrait of a Lawyer as a Young Dad," was written specifically for this project, and is one component in a body of creative work she produced during a recent twelve-month sabbatical.

Jessica Lee
I was divorced and my daughter Angela was on her own when I realized I had another entirely new life ahead of me if I wanted it. So, I quit my job to become a poor student and I couldn't be happier with the decision. My first love is writing, but hopefully, I will do post-graduate work in aging. "Tomato Soup Feelings" is the first memoir in a series that evolved from a growing personal need to trace my emotions.

Janice Levy
Janice Levy has had numerous short stories published in various literary magazines. Her work appears in the anthologies *Lovers* (Crossing Press), *The Time Of Our Lives* (Crossing Press), and *If I Had My Life To Live Over, I Would Pick Daisies*

(Papier Mache Press). She has won the 1992 Painted Hills Literary Award for fiction. A short story of hers has been nominated for the 1993 Pushcart Prize. Her juvenile fiction has appeared in such publications as *Seventeen*, *Child Life Magazine*, *Lollipops Magazine*, and *Long Island Parent*. She is a former Spanish and English-As-A-Second-Language teacher living in New York with her husband and two children.

Mike Lipstock
Mike Lipstock's stories have been published widely in *Nexus*, *Innisfree*, *Sea Frontiers*, *Snowy Egret*, and others. He is presently working on a screenplay. He lives in Jericho, New York, and spends his winters in North Palm Beach, Florida.

Elisavietta Ritchie
Elisavietta Ritchie has many poetry collections, including *The Arc of the Storm*, and *A Wound-Up Cat and Other Bedtime Stories*, as well as *Flying Time: Stories and Half-Stories*. *Tightening The Circle Over Eel Country* won the Great Lakes Colleges Association's 1975-76 "New Writer's Award for Best First Book of Poetry," and *Raking The Snow* won the 1981-82 Washington Writers' Publishing House competition. Editor of *The Dolphin's Arc: Poems on Endangered Creatures of the Sea* and other books, she has read at the Library of Congress, Harbourfront, and many other venues in North America and abroad. She lives in Toronto and Washington DC.

Nancy Robertson
Nancy Robertson is a writer and photographer who lives in Prince Rupert, British Columbia, for half the year and travels to points south in winters. Her photographs and photo essays appear in a wide variety of publications including *Camera Canada*, *Photo Life*, and *Gallerie: Women's Art*. She had a solo exhibition at the Richmond Gallery in 1991 and recently had a photo awarded "Best Canadian Entry" in an international competition. Her poetry and photographs have been published in *Room of One's Own* and her fiction appears in *Prairie Fire*.

Peter C. Samu

Pete C. Samu practices radiology in Toronto.

William J. Smart

William J. Smart is a Toronto writer and teacher whose fiction and poetry have appeared in a number of periodicals in Canada. He has won the Chatelaine Fiction Competition, and Author's Award from The Foundation for the Advancement of Canadian Letters. His work in teaching includes authorship of texts and articles on curriculum development in media literacy. For his work in teaching, he has earned a Hilroy Fellowship Award and the Etobicoke Award of Excellence for Teaching.

Peter Such

Peter Such is the author of collections of poetry, short stories, and novels, including *Fallout, Riverrun* and *Dolphin's Wake.*

Thomas R. Verny, *M.D., D. Psych., F.R.C.P. (C.),* is a psychiatrist, editor, and author of five books including the internationally acclaimed *The Secret Life of the Unborn Child* (Summit Books). He lives in Toronto, Canada.

Marion Woodman

Marion Woodman is a Jungian analyst in private practice in Toronto. She has published several books: *Addiction to Perfection, The Pregnant Virgin, The Ravaged Bridegroom* and *Leaving My Father's House.*